The Successful Virtual Classroom

HOW TO DESIGN AND FACILITATE INTERACTIVE AND ENGAGING LIVE ONLINE LEARNING

Susannah –
I owe the PREP model idea to you!
Thanks for all of your help with the
book!   Dale Christopher

Darlene Christopher

AMACOM

American Management Association

New York · Atlanta · Brussels · Chicago · Mexico City · San Francisco
Shanghai · Tokyo · Toronto · Washington, D. C.

Bulk discounts available. For details visit:
www.amacombooks.org/go/specialsales
Or contact special sales:
Phone: 800-250-5308
Email: specialsls@amanet.org
View all the AMACOM titles at: www.amacombooks.org
American Management Association: www.amanet.org

This publication is designed to provide accurate and authoritative information in regard to the subject matter covered. It is sold with the understanding that the publisher is not engaged in rendering legal, accounting, or other professional service. If legal advice or other expert assistance is required, the services of a competent professional person should be sought.

Library of Congress Cataloging-in-Publication Data

Christopher, Darlene.
  The successful virtual classroom : how to design and facilitate interactive and engaging live online learning / Darlene Christopher.
    pages cm
    Includes bibliographical references and index.
    ISBN 978-0-8144-3428-4 — ISBN 0-8144-3428-2 — ISBN 978-0-8144-3429-1 1. Employees—Training of—Computer-assisted instruction. 2. Virtual reality in management. I. Title.
    HF5549.5.T7C5853 2015
    658.3'1240402854678—dc23
                                        2014009667

About AMA

American Management Association (www.amanet.org) is a world leader in talent development, advancing the skills of individuals to drive business success. Our mission is to support the goals of individuals and organizations through a complete range of products and services, including classroom and virtual seminars, webcasts, webinars, podcasts, conferences, corporate and government solutions, business books, and research. AMA's approach to improving performance combines experiential learning—learning through doing—with opportunities for ongoing professional growth at every step of one's career journey.

Printing number

10 9 8 7 6 5 4 3 2 1

Contents

APPENDIXES

Foreword

UNLOCKING THE MYSTERIES OF FLAWLESS VIRTUAL TRAINING

For professional trainers seeking to develop and further enhance their expertise and confidence in delivering polished virtual-training events, the opportunities have never been greater.

Even though technology tools have grown more sophisticated, they're only as effective as the professionals using them. Instructional designers and facilitators face rising expectations from organizations large and small, in every sector of the global economy, to bring the virtual classroom to life in high-impact ways, engaging learners with rewarding experiences.

Darlene Christopher's *The Successful Virtual Classroom* guides new and experienced trainers to orchestrate high-impact virtual training. It takes a comprehensive, holistic approach, covering not only the *what*—features, functionality, and team roles—but also the *how*—design, facilitation, and global considerations. *The Successful Virtual Classroom* draws on different types of research, including insights gleaned from the author's interviews with more than 20 chief learning officers and other training professionals at Fortune 500 companies, nonprofit organizations, and the U.S. military.

My 14 years of experience in helping develop and execute thousands of online sessions and in coaching thousands of facilitators, both seasoned and novice, tell me that Christopher's detailed approach is spot on. With just one look at her PREP Model—Plan, Rehearse, Execute, Postsession Review—you'll know you've found a vital companion on your journey toward professional excellence.

Equally valuable is *The Successful Virtual Classroom*'s emphasis on:

- Mastering an expanding array of tools designed specifically to engage the online learner
- Scheduling support staff—producer, instructional designer, and/or IT—to provide extra sets of hands *during* your sessions

The Successful Virtual Classroom also provides easy-to-use templates, including a Sample Session Planner Tool and a Sample Facilitator Guide, that you can adapt for your own needs.

As the reach of online delivery continues to burgeon, whether across town or across the globe, count on the step-by-step guidance in *The Successful Virtual Classroom* to help you ride the wave with confidence. With Christopher's help, you'll soon be successfully planning, developing, and executing outstanding global virtual-training sessions!

Karen Hyder
Online Event Producer and Speaker Coach
The eLearning Guild
Kaleidoscope Training and Consulting

Preface

WHAT IS VIRTUAL CLASSROOM TRAINING?

Training programs have traditionally confined both the instructor and participants to the same room and physical location. Fueled by advancing Internet technologies over the last decade, the boundaries and limitations of face-to-face training have been removed, opening up diverse paradigms of delivering training that fall under the category of virtual classroom training.

So what is virtual classroom training? Virtual classroom training is training that takes place in a virtual environment via the Internet. As compared to face-to-face training, where facilitators and participants come together in the same physical space, facilitators and participants in the virtual classroom come together via computer in an Internet-based classroom. Virtual training is also referred to as web conferencing, synchronous learning, or a webinar, and it requires the following hardware and software: a visual display, supplied via a web browser or mobile app, and audio capability, supplied via a conference call or Voice over Internet Protocol (VoIP).

In the course of researching this book, I spoke with a variety of training professionals from chief learning officers and training managers to designers and facilitators to get a true sense of how their training approach has changed in the face of such seemingly limitless solutions fueled by technology. Not surprisingly, the impact has been dramatic. A recurring theme was that conducting in-person training events exclusively was no longer practical or even possible from the standpoint of efficiency, scheduling, or economics. A second theme was that delivering training in the virtual environment is increasingly the most appropriate training solution for meeting current cost and practicality demands.

The structure of workplace teams has also changed. Teams no longer sit within earshot of each other. They are more often geographically dispersed yet collaboratively connected. The topic of virtual classroom training has never been more important because it reflects the way an increasing number of people in organizations really work today. The training professionals I spoke with during my research stressed this reality and why gaining a widespread comfort level with virtual training and team collaboration is essential to the future competiveness of every organization – and the examples are easy to find. Leading companies like Qualcomm gather participants in virtual classrooms across the city of San Diego to work on managerial training. Habitat for Humanity, based in Atlanta, virtually gathers its Latin American-based staff to develop proposal-writing skills. The Army National Guard gathers reserve soldiers virtually to maintain the skills and knowledge of its geographically dispersed on-call workforce. The use of virtual classroom training by these leading organizations is a good representation of the growth in this training delivery method.

TRENDS IN VIRTUAL CLASSROOM TRAINING

The use of virtual classroom training has grown right along with the improving technology that powers it. Each year, the American Society for Training and Development (ASTD) measures the delivery methods organizations use to meet training needs. The 2013 ASTD *State of the Industry Report* found that the percentage of training delivered through a virtual classroom increased 8 percent in 2010 to 10 percent in 2012. The *Corporate Learning Factbook® 2013* (Bersin by Deloitte) reports slightly higher numbers, with 12 percent of total learning hours delivered via virtual instructor-led training and 68 percent of organizations using a virtual classroom tool to deliver learning.

WHY THIS BOOK?

Clearly, the above information shows that delivering training via virtual classroom is not only here to stay, but will continue to grow as organizations strive to stay competitive. As the demand for virtual classroom training increases and this delivery method becomes mainstream, training and development professionals who ignore developing core competencies in this area may find that they are less competitive in the job market.

To create truly engaging virtual classroom training that delivers results, training and development professionals must acquire some new skills and adapt other familiar and long-used skills. In addition to even more attention to preparation and planning, trainers need to meet participants' expectations for content that has been customized and optimized for a virtual classroom. They cannot simply recycle Microsoft PowerPoint presentations and other materials developed for face-to-face classroom environments. What this means for trainers is that the bar for excellence is now set high and that participants expect nothing less than professionally planned, developed, and executed virtual training programs.

GOAL OF THIS BOOK

The goal of this book is to provide facilitators and other training professionals with the baseline tools and techniques to confidently design and facilitate engaging virtual programs that delight learners. This new breed of virtual classroom facilitator must think about every aspect of training from the participant's perspective and then make the appropriate adjustments. Once you, as a trainer, are comfortable with this perspective, you'll have the basic tools to offer this growing method of delivering training to staff in multiple global locations simultaneously and to provide your organization with the ability to respond rapidly to changing market conditions no matter when or where they occur.

WHO SHOULD READ THIS BOOK?

Instructional designers, trainers, and facilitators currently designing and delivering training in a virtual classroom and those wishing to move from traditional face-to-face training to a virtual classroom environment will benefit from this book. As such, this guide will help trainers who are new to virtual classroom training to become proficient and those considered proficient virtual trainers to advance to the expert level.

This book covers a full range of techniques using virtual classroom training, so if you are an experienced online facilitator or producer, the book will serve to reinforce what you already know about the virtual classroom and give you new ideas to make your own programs more engaging and effective.

Specialists in self-paced e-learning and other training professionals familiar with the virtual environment will be able to use this book to expand and enrich their knowledge and skills. Instructional designers considering the use of "blended" solutions in their design will also find this book a useful decision-making resource.

HOW THIS BOOK IS ORGANIZED

This book contains three sections: Getting Started, The PREP Model, and Fine-Tuning. Section 1, Getting Started, offers readers the technical and instructional fundamentals of virtual classroom training. Section 2, The PREP Model, walks the reader through a virtual classroom implementation model that includes all key aspects from roles and content creation to logistics and facilitation. Section 3, Fine-Tuning, shows how to fine-tune virtual classroom training sessions. Content provided here includes additional options for participant interaction, how to work with global participants, and other ways to use the virtual classroom in addition to training sessions.

While each chapter logically flows from one to the next, each chapter is also self-contained, so you can skip to the section you are most interested in exploring. Tips and examples from a wide variety of organizations are also provided throughout, as are references for further information. In addition, Chapters 3 to 10 conclude with a Continuous Learning section for further reflection. Much of the information provided in this book requires both reflection and practical application to the reader's environment to gain a full understanding. The reader is encouraged to make use of the worksheets and checklists on the book's dedicated website, successfulvirtualclassroom.com.

ACKNOWLEDGMENTS

Writing a book is like running a marathon—it requires time, discipline, focus, and support to get to the finish line. I would like to express my deepest gratitude to the many people who saw me through this book. Without your constant help and feedback, this book would not have been possible. Thank you to Patty Barnard, Sandy Cutshall, Susannah Harris, Rick Housler, Peggy Mengel, Eileen Murphy, Michael Randel, and Barbara Brady, for your ideas, feedback, edits, and above all friendship.

To Lucy Bassett, Josebe Bilbao-Henry, Dan Bliton, Roger Courville, Andrea Edmunson, Charles Gluck, Meredith MacDonald Ferris, Sharon Fratta-Hill, John L. Hall, Michelle Hall, Anna Heinrich, Karl Kapp, Adrienne Loder, Debra Moore, Lina Maria Obando M., Peggy Page, Dana Peters, Thomas Perison, Anne Schwartz, Todd Slater, Nick van Dam, Shahron Williams van Rooij, and Stephanie Zaitsev for sharing your best practices and insights into the challenges facing organizations, trainers, and instructional designers who serve an increasingly international and virtual workforce.

To authors who have contributed to the ongoing body of knowledge surrounding virtual training, including Cynthia Clay, Jennifer Hoffmann, Karen Hyder, Cindy Huggett, Nanette Miner, and Becky Pike Pluth. Your groundbreaking work created a solid foundation of information on virtual training upon which I was able to build.

To local Washington, DC, friends and authors Halelly Azulay, Diane Elkins, Karen Mack, and Kathy Reiffenstein. You inspired and supported me when the idea for this book arose.

Thank you to Mark Morrow, an amazing agent and editor whose wisdom and ideas helped the book come together. And thank you to Christina Parisi at AMACOM, who liked the idea for this book and gave me the opportunity to publish it.

Finally, to Mike Christopher, who encouraged me every step of the way and to Mike and Valerie, who generously gave me the time and space I needed to write.

Getting Started

ONE

Introduction

Virtual learning, in the space of just a few years, has greatly enhanced its position as a learning solution among a growing number of organizations. Behind virtual learning's rise in such a short span of time is better, more reliable delivery technology and an increasing number of tech-savvy learners. In addition, the great economic meltdown that began in late 2007 forced companies to find cost-saving alternatives to traditional classroom training.

But whether this shift is driven by cost-cutting business imperatives or strategically nuanced decision-making encouraged by improved technology options and a more accepting workforce, companies are choosing virtual learning solutions in greater numbers than ever. Still, for many training and learning professionals, virtual learning remains an uncertain option for a whole host of reasons. A few of them are fact, but most are fiction.

This book is designed to carefully pick apart the underlying assumptions and misconceptions about virtual learning by providing a range of field-tested tools, tips, and techniques that ensure learner value and keep trainees engaged with a learning event even if the facilitator is in another state, region, or country.

Yes, virtual learning does still have some flaws and limitations, and these shortcomings are what critics point to as they dismiss virtual classroom training as a viable training solution. It's boring, these critics say, or virtual learning audiences don't pay attention and use the time to catch up on email. While these criticisms do reflect a small slice of reality on some level, my opinion of virtual learning is obviously a little more balanced.

AN ENDORSEMENT OF VIRTUAL LEARNING

In the case of virtual classroom training (and face-to-face classroom training for that matter), the magic is not found in the sophistication of the technology but in how well the physical and virtual tools are used to create and facilitate an engaging learning event. The same technology that's behind highly interactive, engaging, and interesting virtual learning experiences is what also creates ineffective and boring virtual training solutions that invite criticism.

You can suffer a "death by PowerPoint" experience virtually or in person. The only differentiator between a successful or unsuccessful training event is good design executed by a skilled facilitator. It's all about creating an ideal mix of appropriate technology, excellent design, and engaging facilitation. If this book has one main goal, it's to guide you toward always hitting that ideal learning mix.

HOW VIRTUAL TRAINING COMPARES
TO OTHER TYPES OF TRAINING

First, virtual classroom training combines elements of traditional face-to-face training with elements of self-paced e-learning. As such, face-to-face and virtual classroom training both require facilitators. Like self-paced e-learning, a reliable Internet connection is needed to connect learners in different countries, regions, or time zones. Table 1-1 compares several components of three types of training delivery.

Many elements of face-to-face and virtual classroom learning also align. Figures 1-1 and 1-2 show typical face-to-face and virtual classroom setups respectively. Note how the group dynamics in the classroom setting—participant discussion led by a facilitator with support materials—are replicated in the virtual setting to achieve the same group dynamics.

Table 1-1 Virtual Classroom Training Compared to Other Types of Training

Component	Traditional Face-to-Face Training	Self-Paced e-Learning	Virtual Classroom Training
Information Flow	Two-way information flow between facilitator and learners	One-way information flow between technology and learner	Two–way information flow between facilitator and learners
Facilitator	Physically present with participants	Not applicable	Physically separated from participants
Location	Physical classroom or meeting room	Accessed via a computer or mobile device	Accessed via a computer and sometimes a mobile device
Materials	Handed out during class	Downloaded from course site	Emailed or mailed to participants in advance or downloaded from virtual classroom
Typical Exercises	Facilitated discussion; small group work	Drag and drop exercises; online simulations	Facilitated discussion; small group work in breakout rooms and polls
Duration	Varies from an hour to multiple days	Modules broken in to small chunks of time, such as 30 minutes	Typically chunked into 60–90 minute sessions

The facilitator's role and responsibilities in a virtual classroom are similar to what you'd expect a facilitator to do in a physical classroom. They include basic tasks, such as:

- Navigating through course slides and other materials
- Facilitating and encouraging interaction among participants through questions and dialogue

Of course, the obvious difference is that the learners experience the virtual facilitator as a displayed static image or a live webcam video feed. Dynamic participant interaction is accomplished via text chats and verbally through a

Figure 1-1 Face-to-face classroom setup.

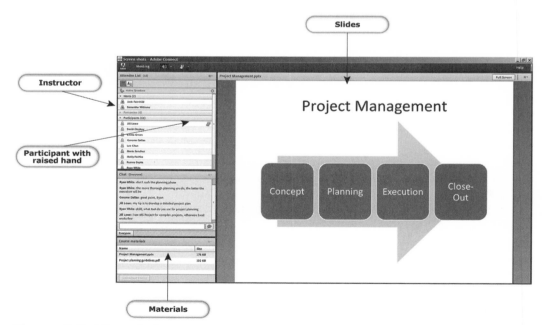

Figure 1-2 Virtual classroom setup.

voice over internet protocol (VoIP) or a teleconference associated with the session. Any notes or points of interest the facilitator wants to emphasize are jotted down on an electronic whiteboard that all the participants see simultaneously. If the facilitator poses a question, the "raised-hand" response serves as a graphic representation associated with the individual learner that appears on the screen. Facilitators have the option of querying all the learners simultaneously using polling tools built into the virtual learning software. Handouts, job aids, and other supplemental material are emailed or posted for participants to download.

WHEN TO USE VIRTUAL CLASSROOM TRAINING

In most cases, answering a few targeted questions about the specific training need, technology available, amount of content, basic participant demographics, and the virtual learning experience of the facilitation team should be enough to determine whether or not virtual classroom training is appropriate for a particular learning program. Here are a few questions you can use to begin this process.

Training Need

- Does virtual classroom training offer a better solution (i.e., more efficient, cost effective, or scalable) for the business need or performance problem than traditional classroom training?
- Does the organizational and learning culture support the use of virtual classroom training?

Technology

- Is the company's virtual classroom tool stable, reliable, and supported by the information technology (IT) department?
- What equipment is available, and is it the right equipment needed to deliver virtual classroom training (i.e., headsets for VoIP and wired Internet connections)?

■ Will the participants have access to appropriately equipped computers, laptops, or tablets, as well as telephones or microphone-enabled headsets?

Content

■ Is it possible to group the content into 60 to 90 minute segments?
■ Does the topic require participant collaboration, interaction, and dialogue?
■ How much time and resources are needed to develop or repurpose face-to-face training for the virtual classroom environment or develop new material for the virtual classroom? Is it possible to do the work and meet the delivery deadline?

Participants

■ Is the environment conducive to virtual classroom training (i.e., private and free from distractions)?
■ Do participants have sufficient technical skills to participate?
■ Are the participants geographically dispersed?

Facilitation Team

■ Are the facilitators skilled in virtual classroom facilitation?
■ What virtual learning support staff can you call on to assist in the session?

Answering these questions provides some initial insight into the appropriateness of a designing a virtual learning solution. Developing questions appropriate for your organizational situation will further refine the broad questions provided here and help you make a final decision about whether to offer a virtual training solution.

Here's additional helpful delivery mode decision-making support. According to the U.S. Distance Learning Association (USDLA), virtual classroom training works best to achieve higher cognitive levels when a synchronous learning environment supports a high level of dialogue and interaction. In other words, don't spend time in the virtual classroom dumping a torrent of information on learners. Instead, use the time to interact with learners to discuss, evaluate, and synthesize information.

Noted adult learning scholar Ruth Clark emphasizes that virtual classroom training is the right choice when learning objectives can be best achieved through:

- Display, explanation, and discussion of relevant visuals
- Interactions using virtual tools, such as polling, writing on whiteboard, and chatting
- Collaborative work among small groups of participants

BENEFITS OF VIRTUAL CLASSROOM TRAINING

As noted earlier, companies are increasingly using virtual classroom training to deliver learning solutions. Additional financial and social benefits driving this increased use are discussed below.

Global Reach

More organizations than ever are using virtual learning to bring individuals and teams together for learning events in an increasingly global business environment. Whether it's a global sales team connecting from offices in different countries or managers separated by multiple zones, the ability to easily connect people and train them in the same virtual classroom is one of the main benefits spurring the increased use of virtual learning. Even facilitators benefit from the technology's reach. Learning sessions may be conducted just as easily whether the facilitator is working from home, office, or any other appropriately equipped location.

Time and Travel Savings

Clearly, virtual learning eliminates the costs associated with traditional classroom learning events, such as travel expenses (airline flights, car rentals, hotel rooms, and meal expenses). For example, if 20 employees need to fly domestically to attend a three-day learning event at a cost of $1,000 each for travel, hotel, and meals, an organization would save $20,000 by delivering the training virtually as a series of short sessions. Costs associated with workflow disruption and lost productivity are also eliminated, since participants join virtual classroom training from their workplaces or home offices. At the same time, virtual training is an efficiency "force multiplier" for facilitators, since they spend more time leading training and less time traveling.

Environmentally Friendly

Since virtual classroom training eliminates the need for air and automobile travel, it's an environmentally friendly alternative to traditional classroom training in which participants and facilitators are geographically dispersed and must travel to the same location. Airplane and automobile emissions are the biggest polluters related to workplace learning. In addition, because training materials may be distributed electronically, virtual training saves paper and, by extension, trees that would be lost by printing materials. For organizations looking to demonstrate their commitment to "green" alternatives and their focus on reducing their carbon footprint, the virtual classroom is an efficiency and public relations win-win.

Chunked Content

According to research published in the *Journal of Applied Psychology*, a distributed approach to learning, where training is delivered as a series of shorter events with time in between, increases learning transfer by 17 percent over a single event. Setting up a series of in-person events for such chunked delivery is often an impractical design option, especially if participants are physically dispersed. However, virtual classroom learning is perfectly suited for delivering a

LINKING VIRTUAL TRAINING TO CARBON EMISSIONS SAVINGS

The World Bank Group strives to be a carbon neutral organization for internal operations. As a knowledge and learning officer, I built the business case for virtual training by connecting it to this corporate initiative.

We are a globally dispersed organization with offices in 110 countries. Bringing trainers and participants to a central hub can, at times, require long flights—a significant source of carbon emissions. Using online tools, I calculated the carbon emissions savings that would be realized by conducting virtual training instead of in-person training, along with savings on travel costs.

Because numbers on carbon emissions don't have meaning for the average person, I used online tools to convert the emissions savings into tangible results, Then, I presented a slide at the beginning of each class showing the amount carbon emissions eliminated by delivering training virtually.

Delivering training in the virtual classroom not only helped the business achieve its goals, but also helped meet our demand for training global staff.

By hosting this session virtually, we avoided 44 tons carbon emissions, which is equivalent to:

- Recycling 20.2 tons of waste
- Growing 1,535 trees for 10 years

TIP

Anna Heinrich, Virtual Classroom Instructional Designer, InSynch Training

What's nice about training people in the virtual classroom is that you can spread out content over time. In traditional training, participants typically only work on skills during the class, not in the learner's true environment where he will be practicing the skills. But, if you design your virtual classroom training as a sequence of short sessions, you can work on a skill in the virtual classroom, then give participants time to practice the skill on the job between sessions. The result is a deeper understanding and discussion of the course content because participants have the opportunity to apply skills on the job between sessions and discuss their experiences during sessions.

---

series of chunked learning events with time in between those events for learners to practice and internalize content.

Security and Weather Disruptions

Virtual classrooms are also immune to disruptions because of changes in airline or train schedules or the closing of major road systems because of political instability, weather, or repairs. Examples of such disruptive events in 2010 include the Arab Spring civil uprisings or the Iceland volcano eruption that spewed engine-killing ash into the jet stream and restricted air travel for weeks.

Virtual training has many advantages over traditional classroom training, from the ability to connect participants globally to reduced travel and lower carbon emissions. Furthermore, the flexibility of the virtual classroom allows trainers to develop shorter segments of content, which helps to improve learning transfer.

THE PREP MODEL

After designing and delivering hundreds of virtual classroom sessions, I developed the PREP Model (Plan, Rehearse, Execute, and Postsession Review). It reflects my practical, real-world, and time-tested approach to virtual classroom

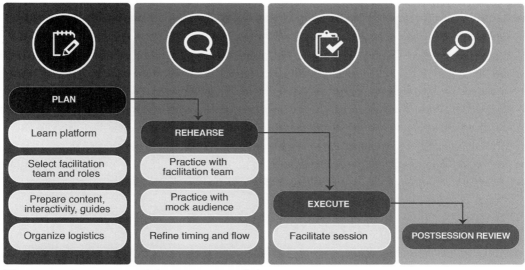

Figure 1-3 Stages of the PREP Model.

training (see Figure 1-3). Even if you have little virtual training experience, you might guess that the model is heavily weighted toward planning. That's because virtual training is a lot like video and audio broadcasting, where many hours are needed to prepare for a broadcast during which disruptions and mistakes are amplified. An unprepared facilitator stumbling through a session saying "umm" constantly can make seconds feel like minutes to the participants, who will interpret the facilitator's lack of preparation and uncertainty as incompetence. Not only does this negatively impact the confidence of the facilitator, but it disrupts the learning process. Following the PREP Model, which will be covered in detail in Section II of this book, will ensure that your virtual classroom design and delivery is flawless. Chapter 7 is dedicated to an explanation of the model.

KEY TERMS

Table 1-2 offers definitions of key terms for the virtual classroom that will help set the stage for this book. For a complete list of virtual classroom terms, see Appendix A.

Table 1-2 Virtual Classroom Terms

Term	Definition
Breakout Rooms	Private meeting subrooms that the facilitator creates for small group work. Participants can have private discussions and collaborate on the whiteboard or chat.
Chat	A feature that allows participants and facilitators to send text messages in real time to chat publicly or privately with others in the classroom.
Drawing and Pointer Tools	A feature that allows the facilitator and participants to graphically mark up the screen in real time when a slide or whiteboard is displayed.
Facilitator	The main speaker, often a subject matter expert, who leads a virtual classroom session.
Instant Feedback	A feature that allows participants to communicate with facilitators at any time throughout a virtual classroom by selecting from a menu of feedback options, such as raise hand, agree, and stepped away. Also referred to as a raise hand feature, status change, or emotion indicator.
Poll	A feature that allows the facilitator to post questions to participants and show poll results in real time or after all responses have been received.
Producer	The virtual classroom technology expert who partners with the facilitator to deliver virtual classroom training.
Screen Sharing	A feature that allows the facilitator or participant to share their own screen, a website, or other application, such as Microsoft Excel, with the class. Also referred to as application sharing.
Voice over Internet Protocol (VoIP)	Instead of using a phone, transmitting voice through the Internet (e.g., Skype).
Whiteboard	A feature that allows for capturing of ideas/information by typing, highlighting, and drawing tools on a digital whiteboard.

CASE STUDIES

A vast array of organizations, from corporations to nonprofit organizations to the U.S. military leverage virtual classroom training to support organizational objectives. Next you will find a series of brief case studies that demonstrate how five organizations—Oracle, The Nature Conservancy, UPS, The Army National Guard, and Deloite Touche Tohmatsu Limited—have used virtual classroom learning in their training and development strategies.

....

Oracle—Bigger Reach and Higher Quality

Reported by John Hall, Senior Vice President, Oracle University

Oracle University first began offering virtual classroom training in 2007. Today, the organization delivers all of its 2,000 courses virtually in 13 languages. According to John Hall, Oracle started offering its courses in the virtual classroom because its 390,000 customers wanted the benefit of time and cost savings offered by virtual training. Oracle's customers also sought virtual learning's broader reach that would allow expanded options for those unable to physically travel to a classroom training event. For example, someone working in Europe can join a virtual classroom that is being conducted during regular business hours in the United States from his home after work.

Hall says the results from the investment in virtual training have been promising. In a recent student satisfaction survey, live virtual classroom training scored two points higher than face-to-face training. Hall reports that the exceptional results are due to the following key factors:

- Courses are supported by a producer focused on any technical issues, so that the instructor can focus on delivering course content.
- Courses are designed specifically for virtual classroom delivery.
- Top instructors have more time to teach since they don't have to travel and, even if an instructor is traveling, classes can continue no matter where the instructor is located.

....

The Nature Conservancy—Mission Alignment

Reported by Todd Slater, Technology Learning Center Program Director, The Nature Conservancy

The Nature Conservancy operates in all 50 U.S. states and in over 30 countries. Since it's such a geographically distributed organization, in-person training is rarely done. According to Todd Slater, virtual training makes sense in terms of cost and efficiency (e.g., no travel costs and better use of staff time) and helps the organization stay mission focused by reducing its carbon footprint. Both of these outcomes are important to a nonprofit organization and its donor and support pool.

Slater also says that virtual classroom training has even more practical benefits—it creates a better learning experience for participants. Staff members are able to learn from a globally dispersed peer group, rather than just those in their immediate area or office. This leads to new perspectives being formed and improves the organization's global effectiveness.

Virtual learning has also changed how the organization delivers training, Slater said. Content is delivered in smaller chunks over an extended period of time. For example, a class might be administered over the course of one to three weeks, so that the learner is online for short periods of time. Self-paced exercises might be included for offline completion, along with a one-hour virtual classroom session that learners can fit into their schedules.

··

United Parcel Service (UPS)—Uniting a Decentralized Learning Community

Reported by Anne Schwartz, Vice President, Global Leadership and Talent Development, UPS

According to Anne Schwartz, the international package delivery giant first considered virtual learning around 2007 to 2008 because traditional classroom training could not meet the demand for their training needs. In addition, Schwarz said that serious consideration of virtual learning was directly connected to technological advancements that allowed training generalists to easily create and deploy rich and effective training. Specifically, these improvements included virtual classroom tools that allow for an interactive and engaging experience with high-quality audio and video, breakout rooms, and chat and assessment capabilities.

Schwartz advises companies thinking about deploying virtual learning to identify early adopter departments or divisions and to consider what type of training is most appropriate for virtual learning. Next, she said that UPS asked 40 global learning professionals to evaluate three web conferencing platforms for functionality and ease of use. After selecting the platform, UPS gave licenses to the selected business unit learning leaders and asked them to pilot a training program for employees. Because UPS has a decentralized learning community, the business units picked the topic, created and deployed the training, and measured the business results.

In one of the first pilots, automotive learning leaders hosted 27 classes in two weeks with 450 attendees. Although the training team spent extra time developing the virtual course, they ultimately saved time due to reduced travel time. When the results of virtual training were compared with face-to-face training, it was determined that virtual learning saved two weeks of time due to reduced travel time, while achieving the same results as traditional training.

Schwartz says that UPS now uses virtual classroom training to teach mechanics and automotive management, telephone service center employees, sales, international management, and many other employees about topics once learned only in physical classrooms.

Army National Guard—Versatility and Access for Citizen-Soldiers®

Reported by Colonel Thomas Perison, former Chief of Training Division for the National Guard Bureau (2012–2013)

Members of the Army National Guard are Citizen-Soldiers® who hold civilian jobs or attend college while maintaining their military training part time. They are prepared to be deployed overseas or domestically in the United States. To maintain currency in a particular area, Army National Guard soldiers are required to complete 39 to 60 days of training per year, depending on their specialty. Training may consist of a combination of hands on, self-paced distance learning, and virtual classroom training. Individual Army National Guard Units also need to maintain a certain percentage of soldiers with a particular skill set, and training can reach many more soldiers when delivered virtually.

Perison reports that virtual classroom training is a great tool because time constraints can be minimized. Since soldiers don't have to travel to attend training, they can actually get more of it. It's not cheaper to develop training for the virtual classroom, but it saves time, which is the biggest constraint. Furthermore, since Army National Guard soldiers also work, the impact to employers is also reduced because soldiers can join a virtual classroom training session after work instead of taking time off from work to travel to a training center.

Deloite Touche Tohmatsu Limited—Connecting Staff and Senior Partners

Reported by Nick van Dam PhD, Chief Learning Officer in Global Talent, Deloitte Touche Tohmatsu Limited

Deloitte Touch Tohmatsu has used virtual classrooms since 2001, but its use has increased significantly in recent years. According to Nick van Dam, virtual classrooms are used to build competencies for all career levels at Deloitte. Learning events focus on the inherent collaborative and social learning functionality in virtual classroom learning.

With its staff of 200,000 globally dispersed employees, a tremendous advantage of virtual classroom learning is vital staff connections that would be impossible to make through physical classrooms only. For example, the company offers a year-long leadership course that includes virtual classroom, in-person, self-paced videos, coaching, and mentoring.

A senior leader, such as a tax professional in The Netherlands, might begin the training journey with the learners by inviting them to the virtual classroom session. During the session, the leaders offer their views on leadership theories and put forth best practices they have found effective in the organization. This virtual classroom session offers a unique opportunity for staff in the leadership program to get to know senior partners personally.

References

American Society for Training and Development (ASTD). *2013 State of the Industry Report*. Alexandria, VA: ASTD Press, 2013.

American Society for Training and Development (ASTD). *Learning's Role in Globally Dispersed Workforces: An ASTD Research Study*. Alexandria, VA: ASTD Press, 2008.

Clark, Ruth. "Four Steps to Effective Virtual Classroom Training." *Learning Solutions Magazine*, May 16, 2005. Retrieved on August 9, 2013, from www.elearningguild.com.

Donovan, John J. and Radosevich, David J. *"A Meta-Analytic Review of the Distribution of Practice Effect: Now You See it, Now You Don't."* Journal of Applied Psychology (1999), 84(5), 795–805.

Driscoll, Margaret and Saul Carliner. *Advanced Web-Based Training Strategies*, San Francisco, CA: Pfeiffer, 2005.

Holden, Jolly T. and Philip J.-L. Westfall. *An Instructional Media Selection Guide for Distance Learning*. Retrieved on October 10, 2013, from www.usdla.org.

Jarventaus, Jenni. "Training a Green Workforce," *T&D Magazine*, September 2007, 28–34.

O'Leonard, Karen. *The Corporate Learning Factbook®2013*. Retrieved on September 22, 2013, from www.bersin.com.

Smolen, Temple. "Building the Business Case for e-Learning," *eLearning Guild Research*, Retrieved on September 22, 2013, from www.elearningguild.com.

Wexler, Steve. *360 Report on Synchronous Learning Systems*. Retrieved on November 1, 2013, from www.elearningguild.com.

TWO

Key Features of a Virtual Classroom

HERE'S HOW TO:

- Use the eight common features of a virtual classroom.
- Associate common features of a virtual classroom with those of a physical classroom.
- Compare how the facilitator and participant use common virtual classroom features to interact.

The first step in successfully designing and facilitating interactive virtual training is developing an understanding of the virtual classroom's key features and how they work. This chapter describes each of these features and their similarity to face-to-face training. It then provides suggestions on how to use these features to interact with learners.

EIGHT COMMON FEATURES

Depending on the vendor, the available features and functionality in virtual classroom training tools are quite diverse, yet most training tools have several common features (see Appendix B for resources on some of the most recognizable virtual classroom vendors).

Here are the eight most common features:

1. Content sharing
2. Screen sharing
3. Audio
4. Chat
5. Drawing and pointer tools
6. Polls
7. Instant feedback
8. Breakout rooms

Why do these eight common features of a virtual classroom matter? Because experienced facilitators who use them correctly are able to deliver virtual classroom training that is as effective as face-to-face classroom instruction. And, according to research by The eLearning Guild on Synchronous Learning Systems, experienced facilitators are able to use these features just like top-notch face-to-face classroom facilitators, who maximize meeting room space by projecting content slides, focusing attention by using flip charts, and creating interactivity and interaction using round table discussion. Let's look at these features in depth.

Content Sharing

The content sharing feature of a virtual classroom tool is the main part of the screen that displays content for viewing by participants. In the content sharing area, the facilitator may display PowerPoint slides, PDFs, video files, audio files, and image files.

Similarity to a Face-to-Face Setting
In a traditional classroom setting, participants see the facilitator, who may use slides, a website, or other information projected on a screen. In a virtual classroom setting, participants focus on the screen and the content shared with

> ## TIP
> For a personal touch, display an image of the speaker in the content area.

them. This keeps participants' attention in concert with the voice of the facilitator. In some cases, the facilitator may also use a webcam, which is covered later in this chapter.

How It Works

Throughout the session, the facilitator clicks through slides in the content sharing area while speaking and interacting with participants. Or, the facilitator may choose to display a brief video in the content area. Most tools also allow the facilitator to open a blank whiteboard in the main part of the screen, the equivalent of a flip chart in a traditional classroom. Using the drawing tools (described later), the facilitator may write on the whiteboard or on the slides to brainstorm with the learners or highlight key concepts.

Screen Sharing

The screen sharing feature allows the facilitator to share her own computer screen with the virtual classroom participants. Facilitators might use this feature to navigate to a file located on their computer desktop or to demonstrate the functionality of a software program (known as application sharing). See Figure 2-1 for an example of how to launch the screen sharing feature. Note that this is one-way sharing—participants don't have the ability to navigate on the facilitator's screen, nor does the facilitator have access to the participants' screens.

Similarity to a Face-to-Face Setting

Some learning labs for computer application training allow the facilitator to display the facilitator's screen on all participant monitors, so that the instructor can demonstrate how to use a software application or navigate to a website.

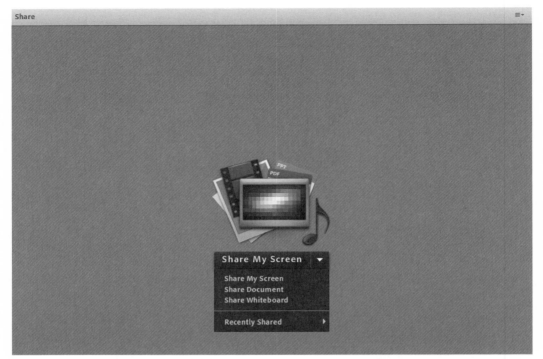

Figure 2-1 Adobe Connect screen sharing. (All Adobe® product screen shot(s) are reprinted with permission from Adobe Systems Incorporated.)

Facilitators who may have taught in a computer lab will be able to apply this experience when using the screen sharing feature in a virtual classroom.

How It Works

Similar to the facilitator's role in a computer learning lab, the virtual classroom facilitator controls the screen and participants watch as the facilitator demonstrates how to perform specific tasks online. Screen sharing is useful to show a website or other content to participants on the facilitator's computer instead of through static screen shots. Each participant's screen follows in real time as the facilitator clicks or scrolls through pages. The facilitator might also use this feature to show participants a completed exercise in an Excel spreadsheet pass control and ask a participant to show his or her screen with the completed Excel spreadsheet. See Table 2-1 for examples of the screen sharing feature.

Table 2-1 Screen Sharing Examples

Facilitator Shares A...	Examples
Website	How to use features and locate content on the Internet, onboarding portal, or collaboration site
Software Application	How to use a feature of a project management tool or budgeting tool
File	How to use a formula in an Excel spreadsheet or a feature in Word

A facilitator might also choose to toggle between the content and screen sharing features. For example, the facilitator might show a slide in the content area with three key points to keep in mind when writing concisely. Then, the facilitator can toggle to the screen sharing feature, open a Microsoft Word document, and show a live demonstration of how to edit a paragraph of text. When the editing demonstration is complete, the facilitator might toggle back to the content area and display instructions on a slide for a similar editing exercise for the participants. Toggling back and forth between screens requires some practice, but the specific techniques are covered in Chapter 6, "Facilitation Techniques."

Audio

Since facilitators and participants are physically separated, a virtual classroom must obviously support voice communication.

Similarity to a Face-to-Face Setting

In a virtual classroom, just as in a traditional classroom, facilitators and participants discuss various topics and questions. At other times participants may listen to an expert describe a problem or demonstrate a process.

How It Works

Most tools offer a choice for audio. Typical audio options are VoIP, built-in teleconference functionality, or both. The audio option is either two-way—both the facilitator and participant can hear and respond—or one-way—the facilitator speaks and participants can only listen. See Table 2-2 for a description of audio options.

Table 2-2 Audio Options for Virtual Classrooms

Audio Option	Description
Two-Way Teleconference	Facilitators and participants use a phone to connect to a conference call. Both facilitators and participants use the phone to speak and listen to each other.
One-Way Teleconference	Facilitators and participants use a phone to connect to a conference call. Facilitators speak on the phone, and participants are in listen-only mode. Intead of speaking, participants use the chat area to type messages to facilitators and other pariticpants.
Two-Way VoIP	Both facilitators and participants use a computer headset/microphone to speak and listen to each other.
One-Way VoIP	Facilitators speak through a computer headset/microphone, and participants are in listen-only mode. Instead of speaking, participants use the chat area to type messages to facilitators and other participants.
Integrated Teleconference and VoIP	Facilitators and participants chose either teleconference or VoIP for audio. May be one-way or two-way.

Participants and facilitators will need a good Internet connection to use VoIP successfully. If both audio and video (via webcam) will be transmitted, the connection will need to be even more robust.

Audio functionality will have a direct impact on the design and facilitation of your virtual classroom training, so it's important to understand your options. For example, if your course design calls for an in-depth discussion of a nuanced topic, a two-way teleconference or two-way VoIP is important. If the

---

TIP

Adrienne Loder, Senior Learning Specialist, Qualcomm

One the first things we learned when we started delivering training in the virtual classroom is the importance of displaying a first-rate image and eliminating ambient noise in the room. Invest in a quality webcam and headset microphone in order to deliver training that looks and sounds professional.

training design requires participants to interact in a way that does not require much conversation and interaction and a chat function will suffice, then a one-way teleconference or one-way VoIP may be the right choice.

Chat

The chat feature allows participants and facilitators to send text messages in real time to each other in a virtual classroom. This feature is similar to the instant messaging offered by Skype or Google Chat. See Figure 2-2 for an example of the chat feature.

Similarity to a Face-to-Face Setting

Just as ongoing question-and-answer sessions help keep training interaction in a traditional classroom lively, the chat feature serves the same purpose to connect and engage the participants with the content in a virtual classroom.

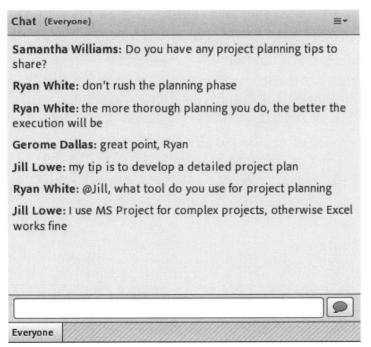

Figure 2-2 Adobe Connect chat feature.

> ## TIP
> You can use the chat feature to replicate the unstructured conversation that takes place before a course starts by greeting participants in chat as they arrive and encouraging small talk.

For example, you can use the chat feature to collect questions or responses to questions just as a facilitator might do in a face-to-face setting when participants raise their hands and answer questions verbally. Participants simply type their questions in the chat area or type responses to questions the facilitator poses verbally.

How It Works

Participants ask questions or share comments by typing into the chat area throughout the session. The name of the participant or facilitator is displayed next to their chat message, so the author of the message is clear to learners and facilitators alike. Both participants and facilitators have the ability to chat privately with individuals or chat publically with the entire group.

The facilitator often reads questions or comments typed in the chat area and responds verbally, since it's difficult to speak and type at the same time. If the facilitator is working with a cofacilitator or producer, this training partner may assist by typing comments or responses in the chat area. More details about the producer role and how the facilitator and producer work together are covered in Chapter 4, "The Virtual Classroom Team and the Members' Roles."

Drawing and Pointer Tools

The drawing and pointer tools allow the facilitator and participants to graphically markup the screen in real time when a slide or a whiteboard is displayed. The drawing and pointer tools work in conjunction with the content sharing feature described earlier. See Figure 2-3 for an example of the drawing tool used to highlight part of a slide.

Figure 2-3 Adobe Connect drawing tool on a slide in the content area.

Similarity to a Face-to-Face Setting

Drawing and pointer tools are the virtual equivalent of capturing notes on a flip chart. They are used to illustrate concepts or capture notes in the same way. You might also compare this tool to how a facilitator uses a laser pointer in a classroom to identify key areas of a projected slide or how a sports analyst on TV uses a telestrator to draw freehand on a screen to analyze a play.

How It Works

The drawing tools are usually represented on a toolbar by an icon that includes a pencil or highlighter for freehand writing and a text tool for typing. The toolbar is usually displayed along with slides or a whiteboard on the main part of the screen so that the facilitator can use the tool to highlight, circle, write text, and so on.

As the facilitator uses the drawing tool, the participants see the changes in real time, but any changes made to either a slide or text don't affect the original slide or content, and these changes are easily erased.

The facilitator can also give participants access to the drawing and pointer tools to write answers to a question or point to part of the screen to answer a question, for example.

Polls

The polling feature allows the facilitator to post questions to participants and show poll results, either in real time or after all responses have been received. Polling can reveal interesting information about the audience's background or knowledge level, as well as opinions on your session's topic.

Similarity to a Face-to-Face Setting

A key difference between asking a question in a physical classroom and virtually is that when polling (or asking and receiving answers to questions) in a virtual classroom, individual participants cannot see the responses of other participants in the session. This "anonymous" questioning is an essential feature of virtual training software, as it encourages participation, protects privacy, and increases response rates.

How It Works

When a facilitator presents or posts a poll with an associated answer set, both the participants and the facilitator are able to watch as the poll results are tallied and displayed in real time. See Figure 2-4 for an example of the polling feature. The facilitator may also choose to display results only after all responses have been collected. Polls are especially helpful for participants who are shy or less confident and therefore may be reluctant to speak or type in the chat box but will eagerly respond to a poll. Polling is also scalable to just about any audience size whether you have an audience of 5 or 500.

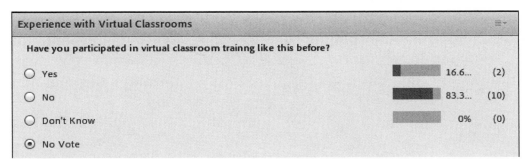

Figure 2-4 Adobe Connect poll feature.

Instant Feedback

Depending on which virtual classroom tool you use, the instant feedback feature might be called a "raise hand" feature, "status change," or "emotion indicator." This feature allows the participant to communicate with instructors at any time throughout a virtual classroom session without interrupting the flow of the instruction by selecting from a menu of feedback options. The type of instant feedback that participants are able to select varies, depending on the virtual classroom tool. See Figure 2-5 for an example of the types of instant feedback participants can provide.

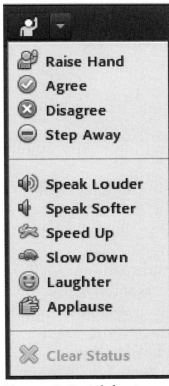

Figure 2-5 Adobe Connect instant feedback options.

Similarity to a Face-to-Face Setting

The most obvious similarity to a physical classroom is when a participant raises her hand or uses other nonverbal communication, such as putting her hand near her ear to indicate that the facilitator should speak louder. The virtual instant feedback feature allows participants to communicate their status via a menu of options. They may select a status to raise their hand or even a status indicating that they are smiling or applauding. Participants can use this feature to replace the normal body language signals that pass between the facilitator and participants.

How It Works

Participants may use the instant feedback on their own or when prompted by the facilitator. When participants select an icon to give feedback, that icon appears next to their name for all others to see. Participants commonly use instant feedback to raise their hands when they have a question, and they wait for the facilitator to acknowledge them so that they can pose the question.

This feature is good to use as an icebreaker for opening a session. The facilitator might ask participants to "raise their hand" if they have lived in another country, and then "call on" one of the responds to explain their experience further. See Figure 2-6 for an example of three participants who selected the raise hand option that appears next to their name.

Once the interaction is complete, the participant lowers her hand or resets her status to neutral. If the participant forgets to reset the status to neutral, the facilitator or producer has enhanced rights to "clear" the status of an individual or the entire class.

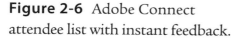

Figure 2-6 Adobe Connect attendee list with instant feedback.

Breakout Rooms

The breakout room feature allows the facilitator to divide participants into small groups to collaborate on a specific exercise. Think of breakout rooms as sub-rooms within the main virtual classroom.

Similarity to a Face-to-Face Setting

Placing participants into breakout rooms in the virtual classroom is just like placing participants in small groups in a face-to-

> **TIP**
> A breakout room allows participants to work in small groups, just as participants work in small groups in a face-to-face setting.

face setting. The facilitator explains the task or exercise that participants need to complete in the breakout room, shares materials such as discussion questions, and informs participants how much time they have to complete the small group work. The facilitator can move from breakout room to breakout room to make sure the breakout groups are working together smoothly and that no group is stuck on the exercise.

How It Works

The facilitator assigns each participant to a breakout room. When the feature is activated, participants are virtually moved into their assigned breakout room. Depending on the assigned task, the participants may work together to brainstorm ideas and write suggestions on a whiteboard. The group might also practice a skill, such as giving performance feedback. Any verbal comments made by the participants in the breakout rooms either over the phone or through VoIP are heard only by those in the breakout room, not by the entire class. When the breakout room group work is done, participants return to the main classroom. If the groups wrote notes in the breakout room, the facilitator may decide to show these notes in the main classroom to debrief the exercise.

FACILITATOR AND PARTICIPANT USE OF KEY VIRTUAL CLASSROOM FEATURES

To understand how the features of the virtual classroom support the instruction, it helps to differentiate how the facilitator and the participants use each feature. Review Table 2-3 to compare how the facilitator and participant use features in the virtual classroom.

Table 2-3 Facilitator vs. Participant Feature Use

Feature	Facilitator (or Producer)	Participant
Audio	Uses phone or computer audio (VoIP) to communicate verbally.	Uses phone or computer audio (VoIP) to listen and may communicate verbally depending on audio setup.
Breakout Rooms	Moves participants into breakout rooms and sets up exercises.	Collaborates with other participants in the same breakout room.
Chat	Writes and reads chat text to check for understanding, answer questions, and give instructions. Writes text to supplement the verbal instructions.	Writes and reads chat text to ask and answer questions, type comments, and read instructions.
Content Area	Displays slides; advances slides.	Views slides.
Drawing and Pointer Tools	Points, draws, or writes on screen.	Points, draws, or writes on screen when such privileges are assigned to participants.
Polls	Posts poll and then posts results.	Casts votes for polls and then views results.
Instant Feedback	Reviews instant feedback. Sets participant status back to neutral.	Clicks on an icon to change status (raise hand, stepped away, etc.).
Screen Sharing	Displays an application or website from his/her desktop in the virtual classroom.	Views application or website and follows navigation.

SAMPLE INTERACTIONS WITH VIRTUAL CLASSROOM FEATURES

The common virtual classroom features just reviewed can be used in a variety of ways to interact with and engage your audience. To give you an idea of how different features can be used to accomplish a similar task, review Table 2-4. It includes examples of how to check audio settings, warm up participants, quiz participants, and check in on completion of an exercise. A description of each sample interaction is described for exercises using the chat, drawing and pointer tool, poll, or instant feedback. If you work with a producer, as described

Table 2-4 Sample Interactions Using Different Virtual Classroom Features

Sample Interaction	Chat	Drawing and Pointer Tool	Poll	Instant Feedback
Audio Check	Facilitator says, "Type yes in chat if you can hear the audio clearly."	Facilitator shows a slide with text "Use your pointer and point to one of the statements below: I can hear the audio clearly; I cannot hear the audio clearly." Facilitator says, "Use your pointer, and point to one of the statements on the screen."	Facilitator posts a poll, verbally asks people to respond to the poll, and continues speaking while the poll is open: I hear the audio clearly (yes, no).	Facilitator says, "Click on raise hand if you can hear the audio clearly."
Warm Up	Facilitator says, "Type your location into chat."	Facilitator shows a slide/image of a map and says, "Use your pointer tool to point to your location on the map."	Facilitator posts a poll and asks participants to respond: Where are you located? Answer set is a list of states, regions, or countries.	Facilitator says, "Click on raise hand if you are participating from your home office today."
Quiz	Facilitator types a statement in chat, reads the statement, and says, "Is this statement true or false: type your answer in chat."	Facilitator posts a slide with a statement. Below it, the words "True" and "False" are displayed. Facilitator reads the statement and says, "Is this statement true or false? Use your pointer tool and point to the word true or false on the screen."	Facilitator posts a poll with a statement and asks participants to respond. Answer set is true, false.	Facilitator posts a slide with a statement and says, "Is this statement true or false? Using the instant feedback feature, select the check mark if true or select the X mark if false."

(continues)

Table 2-4 *continued*

Sample Interaction	Chat	Drawing and Pointer Tool	Poll	Instant Feedback
Exercise Check In	Facilitator says, "When you are done with the exercise, type *done* in chat."	Facilitator posts a slide with the title of the exercise and below it the words "I am done" and "I need more time." Facilitator says, "Use your pointer tool to point to I am done or I need more time on the screen.	Facilitator posts a poll and asks participants to respond. Do you need more time to complete this exercise? Answer set is -No, I am done. -Yes, I need more time.	Facilitator says, "When you are done with the exercise, raise your hand. Keep your hand down if you need more time."

in Chapter 4, "The Virtual Classroom Team and the Members' Roles," the facilitator and producer can share the actions described in the sample interactions.

By comparing how different tasks are accomplished, you will get a sense of the strengths and limitations of each feature. The better you understand how each key feature works, the easier it will be to determine how to use the features to support your design. Throughout this book you will find more examples of how to creatively use these features to interact with and engage your audience.

OTHER FEATURES

It's worth mentioning a few other useful features that some virtual classroom training tools include.

Webcam

Using a webcam during virtual classroom training is similar to using the video feature in Skype. Participants see a small image of the facilitator on their screen during the session and, potentially, their own image broadcast via webcam. Sometimes the facilitator will chose to display her webcam at specific times during a session, such as the opening and closing. Similarly, she may ask participants to display their webcam at certain moments, such as when they ask or answer a question.

File Sharing

If you want to share a file, such as a Word or PDF document, some tools allow these documents to be uploaded and posted in the virtual classroom so participants can download them to their computers.

CONCLUSION

Virtual classroom tools offer a wide range of features and functionality to connect participants and the facilitator. Becoming familiar with these features and how they work is an essential first step for instructional designers, producers, and facilitators. Keep in mind that not all of the features are appropriate for every virtual course, and their use and appropriateness depends on the session's learning objectives and how these features help you achieve specific goals.

References

Barclay, Kathleen, Al Gordon, Jim Hollahan, and Yatman Lai. *The Live E-Learning Cookbook*. Lincoln, NE: iUniverse, Inc., 2003.

Hofmann, Jennifer. *The Synchronous Trainer's Survival Guide*. San Francisco: Pfeiffer, 2004.

Huggett, Cindy. *Virtual Training Basics*. Alexandria, VA: ASTD Press, 2010.

THREE

Getting Started

HERE'S HOW TO:

- Get started in the virtual classroom by becoming familiar with a virtual classroom tool.
- Gain experience in the virtual classroom as a participant.
- Hold low-stakes virtual training sessions to increase your confidence with virtual classrooms.

Learning how to design, deliver, and facilitate truly interactive and engaging virtual classroom training is just like learning any other new skill: it takes practice. In the case of virtual training, you can accelerate the dividends of your practice if you:

- Understand how virtual training is different from classroom training.
- Get comfortable with the use of a few basic technical tools.
- Gain experience from both the participant's and the facilitator's perspective.

This chapter will help you achieve these three goals. In addition, you'll learn some basic guidelines to shorten the ramp-up time you'll need to start using this powerful technology to enhance participants' learning experiences.

This chapter assumes you already have selected a virtual classroom tool to facilitate your training sessions. If your organization is planning to purchase a virtual classroom tool, refer to Appendix C for a table of features to consider when comparing vendors.

STEP 1: **PARTICIPATE IN TUTORIALS AND GATHER INFORMATION**

Goal: Learn About Available Features

Almost every virtual classroom vendor offers free online tutorials (see Appendix B for a list of vendor websites). Take advantage of this resource and participate in live sessions or watch a video recording of an expert user demonstrating the major features of the vendor's virtual classroom tool. When you watch these sessions, note the available features and how to access other key resources. While you're on the vendor's website, download any available tip sheets or reference guides for later use. Reviewing these documents is part of the learning process. Finally, contact your organization's IT or training department and investigate the tools and training materials that have been developed for the virtual classroom tool(s) used by your organization. Once you've gathered this information, make some notes about what your investigation has revealed and then organize and store them for easy access later.

STEP 2: **GET HANDS-ON EXPERIENCE**

Goal: Learn How to Use the Features

Hands-on experience is the best way to learn any new technology. For example, when you learned how to drive a car, you probably spent some time in a classroom studying and reading about how to drive a car and learning the rules of the road. However, it was not until you got behind the wheel of a car and started driving that you truly began acquiring driving skills. While reading books like this one and attending tutorials that explain the various features and functionality of a particular virtual learning technology are good first steps, you also need some practical hands-on experience.

When you are ready for a test run of a virtual classroom tool, position two computers side by side on your desk and log in as the instructor on one computer and as the participant on the other. As you try out the tool's features and functionality on one computer, you'll be able to see how your actions as an instructor are displayed to the participant. Being able to experience these two perspectives simultaneously translates into quicker mastery of the tool and a better understanding of how to use the tool to enhance the virtual learning experience of participants.

Another way to gain hands-on experience is through role play. Ask a colleague to help and alternate playing the instructor and participant roles. While you have the two computers set up, here's a list of basic virtual classroom techniques to experiment with:

- Loading slides
- Advancing slides
- Using drawing tools to annotate slides
- Writing on the whiteboard
- Posting and responding to chat messages
- Sharing your screen
- Launching a poll

TIP

You will gain more if you practice with a colleague at your side than if you practice virtually with a remote colleague because you can compare the instructor and participant views of the virtual classroom. If you aren't side by side, you won't be able to identify the differences in the instructor and participant view. You'll find yourself spending a lot of time describing what you see in order to discover the differences in screens. This can be cumbersome.

By experimenting with these common features, you'll be able to clearly see how an action on the instructor's side requires a response or action on the participant's side. For example, the instructor is offered a poll control dialog box when a poll feature is launched, while the participants are offered a corresponding dialog box that only allows them to cast a vote for a poll.

Use the questions in the checklist in Table 3-1 to guide your learning as you explore the features of a virtual classroom tool and fill in the notes. You can also download this and other practical tools from the book's website, successfulvirtualclassroom.com.

STEP 3: EXPERIENCE THE VIRTUAL CLASSROOM AS A PARTICIPANT

Goal: Reflect on Your Experience as a Virtual Classroom Participant

Experiencing virtual classroom training as a participant is another great way to build your virtual training expertise. You don't necessarily have to pay for a class just to have a practical, real-world experience. Professional associations and vendors offer free webinars on a wide range of topics because they are eager for you to virtually experience their product. Although a webinar is more of a presentation and not typically designed as interactive training, the experience of participating in several virtual sessions is still worth your time, especially if you've had little virtual learning experience.

Depending on the objectives of the session, facilitators will interact with the audience in different ways and use different features of the virtual classroom. Nonetheless, you will get plenty of ideas on what to do and what to avoid. If you see slide designs or an interactive exercise that you like, take a screen capture and save it to your computer for later reference. It's a good idea to keep a journal or reference file to note particularly useful facilitation or interactive design techniques for use when you are ready to design your own course. Use the Virtual Classroom Observation Template in Table 3-2 to capture your reflections on the virtual classes and webinars that you attend.

(*text continues on page 43*)

Table 3-1 Questions to Consider When Learning to Use a Virtual Classroom Tool

Area	Questions to Consider	My Notes
Audio	• What audio options are available? • Can I offer participants the option of VoIP and a tele-phone audio connection or just one or the other? How do I mute/unmute my line and participant audio?	
Breakout Rooms	• How do I move people into and out of breakout rooms? • How does audio work in the breakout rooms? • How does the host move into and out of breakout rooms to check on participants? • Is there a maximum number of breakout rooms? • Is there a maximum number of participants per breakout room? • Can the work that participants do on a whiteboard or other note taking area be brought back into the main classroom screen when the breakout session is over?	
Chat	• Can I send both public and private chat messages? • How do I scroll through the chat messages? • Can I copy and paste text from a Word document or other text file directly into chat? • Can I export the chat?	
Content	• How do I display slides and other content files? • How do I advance slides? • What types of files can I display (eg., .ppt, .pdf, .jpg, .mov)? • How do I delete a file that I upload?	
Drawing & Pointer Tools	• How do I write on the screen or whiteboard? • How do I erase or undo? • What drawing tools are available, other than writing (for example, highlighter tool, stamper tool, ability to draw shapes)? • Is there a pointer tool? • How do I switch from one tool to another?	

Area	Questions to Consider	My Notes
Maximums	• What is the maximum number of participants allowed in a session? • What is the maximum number of hosts (instructors) allowed?	
Plug-Ins	• Does the tool require plug-ins (a small piece of software that provides extra functionality) to be installed in order to work properly? • Do both instructors and participants need to install the plug-in?	
Polls	• What types of poll questions are available (eg., multiple choice, multiple answer). • How do I prepare poll questions in advance? How do I launch/open a poll? • How can I tell how many people have responded to a poll? • How do I share poll results with the audience?	
Screen Sharing	• How do I launch the screen sharing feature? • Can I select a single screen for sharing? • How does the view on the presenter screen differ from the participant screen? • Can participants adjust their screen, for example can they enlarge it? • When I am done using the screen sharing feature, how do I close it?	
Webcam	• How do I start and stop my webcam? • How do participants start and stop their webcam?	
Whiteboard	• How do I open a whiteboard? • How do I write, draw and erase? • How do I give access to the whiteboard to participants?	

Table 3-2 Virtual Classroom Observation Template

Observation Template		
Date:		
Session Title:		
Session Topic:		
Area to Assess	**Reflection Questions**	**My Notes**
Instructions	Was it clear how to access the virtual classroom?	
Opening	Did the session start on time? If not, what was your reaction as a participant? Did the facilitator capture your attention when he began?	
Audio	How was audio transmitted? Was the audio clear? Were there any disruptions?	
Interaction	Which features of the virtual classroom were used during the session? Approximately how often did the facilitator interact with participants? When were you most engaged? When were you least engaged? What interaction techniques were used during the session that you would like to replicate?	
Content/Slides	Was the content on the slides easy to read? Was it properly formatted and visually appealing? What ideas for presenting content would you like to replicate?	
Speaker/ Facilitator	Was the facilitator's voice clear? Was the facilitator enthusiastic? What facilitation techniques did he use that you would like to replicate?	
Facilitation Team	Who else was online during the session to support the speaker? What did they do?	
Closing	How did the facilitator close the session? Was he rushing to finish on time? If so, how did you react as a participant?	
General Notes:		

STEP 4: **HOLD A LOW-STAKES VIRTUAL CLASSROOM SESSION**

Goal: Begin Designing and Facilitating for Virtual Audiences

Now that you've seen the "participant" side of the virtual classroom, it's time to experience the "presenter," or "facilitator," side of a session. If you've completed Steps 1 through 3, you should be comfortable with the virtual classroom tool basics and ready to hold a test virtual meeting with coworkers or friends. Even though it is a low-stakes meeting, prepare as if it were a live, high-stakes session. For example, if a weekly informal conference call or in-person meeting is a regular part of your routine, try holding this meeting virtually.

Since this will be a test session, you can afford to take chances, so think creatively about your meeting and use all the appropriate features of your virtual classroom tool. For example, if the purpose of the meeting is to plan an upcoming workshop, create a poll and have participants vote on their preferred date. Or, use the whiteboard feature to assign tasks in real time to the virtual participants as you agree on roles and responsibilities for the workshop. Create a few well-designed and appealing support slides for the meeting, such as an agenda or topics with questions you want to address.

Next, focus on facilitation techniques in a virtual setting. As you facilitate the session, consider how your audience interactions are different without access to familiar body language cues that we all use to get our message and meaning across to learners.

LOW-STAKES SESSION CHECKLIST

✓ Send log in/audio instructions and observation template to participants.
✓ Prepare agenda, slides and materials.
✓ Prepare interactions with participants.
✓ Hold the low-stakes session.
✓ Review feedback from participants, and determine what further adjustments are needed.

At the end of your low-stakes virtual session, make notes about what went smoothly and where you see room for improvement. Consider sharing an observation template, such as the one in Table 3-2 so participants capture specific feedback for you. Continue your virtual training education by holding other low-stakes sessions until you are completely comfortable with the technology and how to use it effectively.

NOT NEW, JUST USING A NEW VIRTUAL CLASSROOM TOOL

Even experienced virtual classroom designers or facilitators must have a continuous learning mindset since virtual training tools, like any sophisticated technology, are always evolving and improving. All virtual trainers must take a methodical approach to learning how to use new or upgraded technology. The experience is like trading up to a new, technologically advanced phone. All virtual classroom tools offer similar feature sets, but each new version or upgrade is slightly different.

TIP

Cindy Huggett, author of *The Virtual Training Guidebook*

Even if you take a course to become a virtual facilitator, that's not the end of your learning curve. It's important to stay on top of the continuous changes to the virtual classroom platforms that you use. I do this by keeping vendor blogs on an RSS feed, visiting vendor websites, practicing with the platform, participating in LinkedIn groups, and using Twitter to keep up with product updates.

CONCLUSION

The goal of becoming comfortable with a virtual classroom tool is to enable you to focus on your subject matter when delivering training rather than on the technology. In practical terms, this means that you know exactly what will

TRAINING VIRTUAL FACILITATORS AT TD BANK

TD Bank facilitators deliver a variety of company training programs virtually, including interviewing and sales skills, to employees at East Coast retail banks. Peggy Page, Learning Solutions Design Group Manager, developed a two-part process using the Adobe Connect virtual classroom platform to ensure that traditional classroom facilitators are prepared to lead virtual classroom training. Here is a description of the process:

1. Adobe Connect 101: Virtual facilitator trainees begin with a two-hour class covering the key features of Adobe Connect and must pass a "driver's test" to advance to step 2.
2. Virtual Master's Program: Next, the virtual facilitators complete six weekly 90-minute virtual classes with intersession work and practice that includes feedback. Upon completion, facilitators are assigned to facilitate six virtual classes, two of which are observed by a facilitator guru. Using a virtual facilitation skills rubric with performance standards as a guide, the guru observes the new facilitator in areas of technical proficiency and facilitation skills and provides specific feedback.

This methodology has helped TD Bank facilitators successfully transition from traditional classroom training to live online training. Peggy estimates that delivering training via virtual classroom costs about 40 percent less than traditional classroom training. By delivering training in the virtual classroom, TD Bank not only keeps up with the high demand for training but also saves money for the business.

or won't happen to the screen when you click a button or activate a feature so you won't make a mistake in front of a live virtual audience.

Another important reason to learn a virtual classroom tool is to understand the opportunities for interaction and to use as many appropriate features as possible as you build your design and facilitation skills—and ultimately, to enhance the learning experience of your participants. Refer to Appendix D for virtual classroom resources, including books, e-publications, and organizations and professional associations. Use these resources to stay current with virtual classroom developments and ideas to enhance your course design and virtual classroom facilitation techniques.

CONTINUOUS LEARNING

1. Recall a great learning experience you had. What made it great? What elements of that experience can you introduce into your virtual classroom?
2. Attend a tutorial to learn about the features in a virtual classroom tool.
3. Attend virtual classroom training, and use the Virtual Classroom Observation Template (Table 3-2) to capture your reflections on the training.
4. Select a low-stakes meeting to deliver via a virtual classroom.
5. Conduct an Internet search using keywords, such as virtual classroom, synchronous training, or the name of your virtual classroom platform. Look for current articles and blog posts that are interesting to you.
6. Review the Virtual Classroom Vendors in Appendix B and Organizations and Professional Associations in Appendix D. Check the social media resources for each vendor and join or follow the groups that interest you.

References

Huggett, Cindy. *Virtual Training Basics*. Alexandria, VA: ASTD Press, 2010.

Hyder, Karen, et al. *The eLearning Guild's Handbook on Synchronous e-Learning*. Santa Rosa, CA: The eLearning Guild, 2007.

The PREP Model

FOUR

The Virtual Classroom Team and the Members' Roles

HERE'S HOW TO:

- Distinguish the roles of the virtual classroom team members.
- Understand the different skills required for each key team member.

Delivering training in the virtual classroom is best accomplished as a team rather than as a single individual. Now that you understand virtual training's basic architecture and its key functional capabilities, let's explore the various team member roles and responsibilities and what is required to design and develop a typical session. As you might imagine, a virtual training team is similar to a traditional classroom training team.

COMPOSITION OF VIRTUAL CLASSROOM TEAMS

Below you'll find the list of members who play a role in the virtual classroom. See Figure 4-1 for a diagram and read on for a definition of each member's expected role and responsibilities.

- Producer: The virtual classroom expert who provides technical expertise.
- Facilitator: The instructor in charge of leading the session.

- Subject Matter Expert: The team member with the session's relevant content knowledge.
- Instructional Designer: The virtual classroom content designer.
- Administrator: The person who provides administrative support.
- Information Technology (IT) Support: The person who provides technical support.
- Participants: Those enrolled in a session to gain knowledge, skills, and abilities.

Figure 4-1 Members of the virtual classroom team.

Producer

Like a producer on a movie set, a nightly newscast, or a stage production, a virtual classroom producer works behind the scenes during a live session to support the flawless delivery of the event. Jennifer Hofmann, author of *The Synchronous Trainer's Survival Guide*, calls the producer an "extra set of hands" that compensates for the loss of a "set of eyes."

As illustrated in Figure 4-1, the producer role is central to virtual classroom training, as this person orchestrates all the elements. The producer typically works with the facilitator(s) in advance of a session rehearsing and fine-tuning the various technical features, such as polls and online exercises. The producer troubleshoots technical issues during a session in real time and ensures minimal disruption due to technical glitches. If a session involves a subject matter expert, the producer works with that person to test audio connections and explain how the session will run. The producer understands the virtual classroom's technical aspects—how the features work—and can partner with the instructional designer to determine how to best design a session and incorporate interactive features. He also engages with the administrator and IT support to plan the logistics of a session. Finally, the producer interacts with participants as he supports the facilitator and is ready to step in and troubleshoot any problems that participants experience during the live session.

Facilitator

Like the facilitator in a traditional classroom, the facilitator in a virtual classroom is the class leader. She is responsible for the overall content of the session and is often the subject matter expert as well. Alternatively, she may partner with a subject matter expert in the virtual classroom as described below.

Subject Matter Expert

Clearly, this role is similar to the same role in face-to-face classroom training, but virtual classroom training offers new design options. For example, the facilitator might choose to interview the subject matter expert and role play as if she were a talk show host. In this case, the subject matter expert would not be expected to have any particular expertise with the virtual classroom since the role is content centered.

Instructional Designer

The instructional designer's role in face-to-face classroom training mirrors the designer's role in virtual classroom training. The designer is expected to use adult learning principles and build in all the appropriate virtual interactions required to accomplish learning objectives and keep participants engaged in the session. The designer also creates materials for the course such as slides, videos, participant manuals, facilitator guides, and handouts.

Administrator

Virtual classrooms in particular, require well-coordinated logistic and communication support. The administrator enrolls participants, sends class materials, provides log in instructions, and carries out any postsession tasks, such as providing additional learning materials or session evaluation links.

Information Technology (IT) Support

The IT person manages the various technical components that are part of any virtual classroom and ensures that your virtual training tool is upgraded to the latest version and is current on all of your company's servers. IT typically manages the required telephone infrastructure for your virtual training tool.

Participants

The participant role is similar for virtual and classroom training. The difference in virtual training is that participants join a session from their work or home environments, instead of meeting in a training room.

COMMON KEY ROLES

In general, the four roles of producer, facilitator, instructional designer, and administrator are required for successful virtual classroom training. Depending on the type of training you deliver, some of these roles may not be relevant. And, depending on the size of your organization and available resources, your

---

TIP

Sharon Fratta-Hill, PhD, former Vice President of Distance Technology at the Graduate School USA

Graduate School USA provides continuing education for government workers. We converted five traditional training courses to virtual classroom training over four months. We trained our lead instructional designer on quality virtual classroom instruction and then used the ADDIE (analysis, design, development, implementation, evaluation) process for conversion. The department chair or faculty member worked with us in the analysis phase. When we were done converting courses, the instructional designer became the producer for the virtual classroom deliveries.

---

team may consist of several people or a few people playing multiple roles. In addition, since the four roles require specific and complementary skills, the instructional designer may also be the producer or the facilitator may also be the subject matter expert and administrator. In some situations you may be the person who plays all roles! Table 4-1 summarizes the key skill sets for the four key roles. Then, the next section covers the skills and competencies needed by each of the common key roles.

Table 4-1 Skills for the Key Virtual Facilitation Team Members

Producer	Facilitator	Instructional Designer	Administrator
Technology skills	Technology skills	Client engagement skills	Event planning skills
Facilitation skills	Facilitation skills	Writing skills	Communication skills
Multitasking skills	Multitasking skills	Multimedia skills	
Time management skills	Time management skills		
Typing skills	Presentation skills		
	Verbal skills		

Producer

The producer should have experience with the particular virtual classroom tool used for your training session. The most successful producers have the following skills and competencies:

- **Technology Skills:** A producer does not need to be a computer programmer, but a producer should have an interest in technology and have expert knowledge of the virtual classroom tool.
- **Facilitation Skills:** Although the producer is not the main speaker in the virtual classroom, the producer needs basic facilitation skills to communicate effectively with participants.
- **Multitasking Skills:** Since the producer's job is to ensure that all elements of the course are coordinated effectively, multitasking skills are essential. This "ringmaster" may be chatting with an individual participant to solve a technical problem, troubleshooting connectivity issues, launching polls, or preparing a screen for the next exercise.
- **Time Management Skills:** The producer needs a keen awareness of time and timing since part of the job is to work with the facilitator to ensure the session begins and ends on time.
- **Typing Skills:** The producer manages the chat area, answers questions when possible, and refers other questions to the facilitator. All of this activity requires quick, accurate typing while monitoring the screen, so touch typing is essential (i.e., two-finger, hunt-and-peck typing is not an acceptable skill level).

Facilitator

The facilitator needs a wide range of skills as the leader of the virtual classroom session. In addition to a strong command of the session's subject matter, the facilitator must be skilled at virtually engaging participants. Here are the key skills a facilitator needs.

- **Technology Skills:** To focus on teaching the subject matter rather than on the technology, the facilitator must be comfortable with the virtual classroom technology tool they're using. This comfort level will help when planning how to effectively deliver content to participants. A certain amount of interest and curiosity with virtual classroom software is also important, since facilitators may need to work with the producer to solve technical issues.

- **Facilitation Skills:** The facilitator must engage participants with active listening and solicit their contributions through the use of familiar classroom techniques, such as summarizing and paraphrasing participant comments.

- **Multitasking Skills:** The facilitator must be able to jump quickly from one task to another to keep the session moving smoothly, while simultaneously keeping an eye on the other activities on the home screen such as ongoing chats and instant feedback (when participants "raise" their hands to ask questions).

- **Time Management Skills:** Your session is likely squeezed into an already busy work day for participants, so keeping to the schedule is imperative. Participants also have little patience for a facilitator who does not manage time well. Finally, it's not as easy to make up time in a virtual classroom session as it has a less flexible structure than in-person training, so time management skills are essential. Using your facilitator's guide and the support of your producer can help with time management.

- **Presentation Skills:** Many of the presentation skills needed for classroom and virtual training are the same. The facilitator must be comfortable and confident in front of an audience and speak clearly in complete thoughts and phrases. A facilitator must also know how to effectively manage a question-and-answer session.

- **Verbal Skills:** In a face-to-face setting, learners can rely on body language, gestures, facial expressions, and a bit of lip reading to fill in language gaps. In a virtual classroom, these nonverbal cues are limited or absent, so the facilitator needs to speak clearly and precisely to help convey their message. The virtual facilitator should be skilled at making deliberate word choices such as, "Sally, use the phone and tell us your answer to #6" or "Turn to page 9 and spend two minutes reflecting on the text. When you are done, type your response to the question in the chat box." The facilitator should also speak with a variety of vocal tones to keep her voice interesting for participants.

TIP

The facilitator can work with the producer to manage questions throughout a session and during a question-and-answer session if participants use the chat feature. The producer can act as the "voice" of participants and read questions out loud, grouping similar questions together.

Instructional Designer

In addition to specific functional experience and expertise with a virtual training tool, an instructional designer must be able to apply the same familiar and well-understood adult learning principles to virtual training design. This includes learner-centered design that draws on experiences and contributions from participants.

- **Client Engagement Skills:** The instructional designer must be adept at working with a subject matter expert (often the same person as the facilitator) to translate what often amounts to a 'brain dump' into interesting, focused learning materials. Good listening and questioning skills and diplomatic sensibility are key skills for success.
- **Writing Skills:** The writing style of a virtual instructional designer, like that of a traditional classroom designer, must be clear and concise so that slides, workbooks, and instructions are easily understood by virtual training participants.
- **Multimedia Skills:** The designer needs strong multimedia skills to develop materials and select images that are visually appealing for display in a computer screen format.

Administrator

The course administrator provides support to both the facilitation team and participants to ensure the course runs smoothly.

- **Event Planning Skills:** Just like in-person training, virtual classroom training requires good event planning. The administrator should understand the essentials of event planning to manage logistics (where the facilitation team will sit), materials, and course enrollment. The administrator also needs to be organized, resourceful, and detail oriented to make sure that log in instructions for participants are clear and links are correct.
- **Communication Skills:** Good interpersonal skills and a courteous manner are important for the course administrator, since this person may be the first point of contact for session participants. The ability to write and speak clearly is an important skill for this team member.

How the Roles Work Together

Each team member role has specific tasks before, during and after a session. The administrator and instructional designer are active before and after a session, but not during the session. The facilitator and producer, however, have tasks before, during, and after a session. Review the sample breakdown of tasks in Table 4-2 to determine how best to distribute and manage the roles for your virtual classroom session.

The way you distribute the work among these roles will depend on the skill set, experience level, and number of team members. Regardless of how the tasks are divided, it is essential to appreciate the full range of tasks needed and ensure the roles are competently filled. Not only will this work ensure the smooth execution of your virtual training session, but your efforts will also maximize the efficient transfer of knowledge.

How the Facilitator and Producer Work Together

The facilitator and producer roles are most active during a virtual classroom session. These team members work together to deliver the training and engage the audience during the live event. The facilitator speaks, advances the slides, and engages the audience verbally, while the producer monitors the chat, sets up exercises, and polls. The content and complexity of your virtual classroom training will determine the level of expertise needed by this facilitation team. Table 4-3 provides a sample breakdown of tasks performed by this team and will assist you in session planning.

Table 4-2 Breakdown of Tasks for the Key Virtual Classroom Roles

Phase	Task	Role
Before	Design course.	Instructional Designer
	Create course materials, leader guide.	Instructional Designer
	Design course evaluation.	Instructional Designer
	Test materials in virtual classroom.	Producer
	Test features of virtual classroom.	Producer
	Create place for people to enroll in course (learning management system or elsewhere) and communicate instructions to enrollees.	Administrator
	Provide log in instructions to enrollees.	Administrator
	Communicate with participants to explain how to access materials.	Administrator
	Rehearse for session.	Facilitator and Producer
	Develop back up plans.	Facilitator and Producer
During	Facilitate session.	Facilitator
	Support facilitator during session.	Producer
	Present content.	Subject Matter Expert or Facilitator
	Troubleshoot technical issues.	Producer

Phase	Task	Role
After	Edit, post, and/or archive recording of session, if applicable.	Producer
	Send chat transcript to appropriate parties, if applicable.	Producer
	Lead postsession debrief with team.	Facilitator
	Adjust materials, exercises based on postsession debriefing.	Instructional designer
	Adjust layout of room based on postsession debriefing.	Producer
	Follow up on technical problems to learn if they can be prevented in the future.	Producer
	Adjust facilitation technique, flow, and timing based on postsession debriefing.	Facilitator
	Gather evaluation feedback from participants and share with facilitation team.	Administrator
	Send follow-up materials and information to participants.	Administrator

Table 4-3 Facilitator and Producer Tasks During a Virtual Classroom Session

	Facilitator	Producer
General	Main speaker, subject matter expert.	Virtual classroom expert. May or may not be familiar with subject.
Slides/Content	Advances slides. Engages audience verbally.	Explains technical features. May kick off and conclude the session.
Chat	Not active in chat. Comments verbally on what others type.	Active in chat. Engages audience by posting and responding to questions/comments. Prompts facilitator to address chat questions that are subject matter specific. Types key messages to reinforce learning as facilitator speaks.
Polls	Comments on poll results.	Opens/closes polls.
Exercises	Leads and debriefs exercises.	Explains how exercises will run.

LOCATION OF FACILITATION TEAM

Ideally, the producer and facilitator should be in the same location to deliver a training session. When the facilitation team is in the same space, the members can mute the audio and troubleshoot issues if necessary or use hand gestures to communicate critical information that ultimately supports smooth classroom operations and the learning experience.

However, it's not always possible for this essential team to be in the same physical location. When facilitation team members cannot be in the same location, take the following actions to make the best of the situation:

- Rehearse thoroughly with the facilitation team.
- Keep a separate instant messaging tool open (such as Skype), so you can communicate privately outside of the virtual meeting room. (It may also be possible to send private messages through your virtual classroom tool, but have a back-up messaging tool ready as well.)
- Exchange phone numbers so you can get in touch with one another in an emergency.

TIP

Meredith MacDonald Ferris, Organization Development and Trainer Consultant from the Training Resources Group

Whenever possible, the facilitator and the producer should be in the same room. The close proximity of another "live" person makes it easier for the facilitator to speak as if addressing a physically present audience rather than just a computer monitor.

LOCATION OF LEARNERS

While it may be tempting to invite learners into the facilitation room during the live session, if some of them are in that location, it may be difficult to manage. The needs of an in-person learner are different from those of a virtual learner and mixing the two means that one of the two audiences will suffer. Learners in the room may divert the facilitator's attention from the screen. Furthermore, audio challenges arise with learners in the room. If you are using a conference call and speakerphone, virtual learners may be able to hear the facilitator clearly but will not hear when in-person learners speak if they aren't sitting by the phone.

A highly skilled and experienced facilitation team may have the experience to manage the two groups and the challenges they present by engaging both groups equally and weaving their participation into the session. But a good strategy is to avoid this practice when you are new. More information on participant logistics is covered in Chapter 5, "Developing Virtual Classroom Training."

A TEAM OF ONE

What if you work in a small training department or deliver virtual classroom training by yourself as an independent contractor? While the situation is not optimal, a solo facilitator can still successfully deliver virtual training. Here are some pointers that may help:

- Prepare clear instructions regarding logistics and test the instructions as if you were a participant to ensure accuracy before sending to participants.
- Mitigate problems in advance by asking participants to check their computers before your session to ensure they have access to your virtual classroom. Even better, call each person and walk them through the process before your course begins. It's much easier to troubleshoot a problem one-on-one ahead of time than during a live session while the rest of the attendees wait.
- Log in early to test all the features of the tool that you will use, including audio, so you can troubleshoot and fix any problems before the start of your session.

- Since it's impossible to present material verbally and type into the chat area at the same time, simply respond to comments or questions verbally.
- If several participants are experiencing the same technical problem, pause the session and troubleshoot.
- Prepare a plan ahead of time to determine what to do if only one person has a technical problem. Perhaps stopping makes sense; perhaps not. If you think through potential technical scenarios that may occur, it will be easier to determine the best action to take.

CONCLUSION

The roles needed to successfully deliver virtual classroom training are similar to traditional classroom training roles with the exception of the producer. Because the producer is the ultimate event orchestrator and problem solver in the virtual classroom, it's essential to the smooth running of your virtual training event that this role be filled, even if the facilitator has to assume this role. In addition, it takes a range of skills to successfully deliver virtual classroom training, from instructional design to time management to technology skills. Assess the skills of team members to ensure you have all skill sets required for successful virtual classroom training.

CONTINUOUS LEARNING

1. Attend virtual classroom training and analyze the role division.
2. Analyze your own resources to put together a virtual facilitation team and compare the skill sets with those in this chapter.

References

Hofmann, Jennifer. *The Synchronous Trainer's Survival Guide*. San Francisco: Pfeiffer, 2004.

Hyder, Karen. "Identifying the Skills and Team Members Needed to Support Synchronous Online Sessions and Webinars," Presented at the eLearning Guild Annual Gathering, Orlando, April 14–17, 2008.

FIVE

Developing Virtual Classroom Training

HERE'S HOW TO:

- Apply design techniques to the virtual classroom.
- Develop compelling matrials for the virtual classroom.
- Create engaging interactions.

Training designed for delivery in the virtual classroom is still training, and the same principles of adult learning and instructional design apply. You need to analyze the nature of the training problem, develop a training design based on clear learning objectives, and create appropriate and effective training materials.

ANALYSIS

Since the basic rules of effective training don't change just because you're delivering the learning content online, it's important to thoroughly analyze what performance gap you're addressing before prescribing a solution. Once you've determined that a performance gap is related to deficiency in skills or knowledge (and not a lack of tools, resources, or motivation), the next step is to determine if a virtual classroom is the most appropriate delivery solution.

The virtual classroom works best when training is collaborative and requires discussion. That's why a blended learning approach is particularly well suited for the virtual classroom. For example, you provide participants with prereading, self-paced e-learning, or other exercises that provide introductory material. Then, the participants spend time in the virtual classroom discussing, collaborating, and applying the introductory material to real life. Salman Khan, founder of the Khan Academy, a not-for-profit organization that offers an educational video library on hundreds of topics, champions the flipped classroom model. In this model, online lectures are assigned as homework; review of homework and discussions are then part of the classroom activities, so the instructor and peers can help problem solve and exchange feedback.

After deciding that the virtual classroom is an appropriate delivery solution, gather information about the target population's learning needs. Ask those familiar with the target population—managers, supervisors, and others—about the most frequently asked questions or most commonly made mistakes. If your target audience includes people from different cultures, refer to Chapter 8, "Working with Global Participants."

Next, analyze the learner's environment. Find out if learners have access to a physical location appropriate for participation in virtual classroom training (i.e., a location with the right equipment and Internet access that is free from distractions). For example, if your target audience works in a retail business

ANALYSIS QUESTIONS TO ASK

- What is the performance gap I am trying to solve?
- Does the content require collaboration and discussion with a facilitator and peers?
- Is my target population familiar with the subject matter?
- What learning need does my target population have?
- What cultural considerations do I need to keep in mind?
- Does my target population have access to the right equipment and environment for virtual classroom training?
- What stakeholders do I need to engage?

and the only computers with Internet access are in constant use by sales associates, then obviously this is not a good environment for virtual classroom training.

Finally, conduct a stakeholder analysis and determine who needs to be informed, influenced, or queried to make training a supported success. Consider speaking to:

- **Managers:** Get manager input on the training need and ensure a commitment to follow through on support.
- **Information Technology (IT) Support:** Get input from the technical staff regarding potential issues that might impact the smooth operation of virtual classroom training, including software, plug-in installation, bandwidth constraints, and telephone integration.
- **Facilities Staff:** Check with your organization's facilities or administrative staff to determine if a dedicated room is available to serve as a virtual classroom. Check on the room environment including Internet connections, phone access, and relative noise level.
- **Trainers:** Ask other trainers or training team members about any previous experience with virtual classroom training with your target audience or within your organization. Find out what concerns, problems, or best practices emerged from their experience conducting virtual classroom training.

DESIGN

Good design begins with learning objectives that describe specific behaviors or skills that participants are expected to demonstrate upon completion of the course. Like guideposts, all course content and interactivity must support the achievement of these objectives.

Although well-written learning objectives are not unique to virtual classroom training, what *is* different about virtual classroom training is that the instructional designer must think carefully about what's reasonable to accomplish in a virtual classroom setting and develop the objectives accordingly. While it's quite common to design a day long face-to-face training session, virtual classroom sessions are usually about 60- to 90-minutes long. If this limit results in a series of 90-minute sessions, you'll have to align the objectives accordingly.

Time is also precious in the virtual classroom. That's why any extraneous, nice-to-have material should be presented as extra handouts or postcourse work and not included as part of the virtual class. Finally, don't minimize the importance of learning objectives just because you are designing online virtual training. You'll still use learning objectives to select instructional methods and to develop an evaluation strategy for the training event.

Instructional Methods

The instructional methods used for designing virtual classroom training will depend on a variety of factors including the following.

- **Learning Objectives**: If your objective is to teach participants how to use an online tool, then your instructional method might include demonstrations of the tool and self-practice. If the objective is focused on behavioral change, then the design might include role-plays, reflection exercises, and video scenarios.

- **Audience Size**: The design for a small audience of 10 to 20 participants is different than a design for a large audience of 75 to 100 participants. Design for a small audience could include several one-on-one interactions, in which each learner contributes individually to an exercise (such as writing on a whiteboard), or working in small groups in breakout rooms. Activities such as chat exercises or poll questions may be more appropriate for large group interaction.

  Determining an appropriate audience size for a virtual classroom depends on the content being taught. However, a common audience size is between 10 and 20 participants. A small audience offers more personalized interaction among the participants. Online virtual training for a large audience is not a common practice and is mainly associated with a webcast using one-way presentation techniques.

■ **Facilitation Team Composition**: Chapter 4, "The Virtual Classroom Team and the Members' Roles," covered virtual learning that uses both a facilitator and producer. Working together, these two can orchestrate a high level of interaction and maximize the features offered by virtual classroom training software. In contrast, a solo facilitator has more limited options and so must include exercises that a single person can launch and sequence to produce smooth transitions and operation. For example, the facilitator might plan to load a poll or determine breakout room composition while participants work individually on workbook exercises.

■ **Virtual Classroom Tool Features**: While all virtual classroom tools have a common, core set of features and functionality, differences do exist. Some will likely influence your design. For example, if you are using WebEx, participants can be asked to use a pointer tool to identify a displayed answer on the screen, with the participant's name appearing alongside the pointer. However, this type of pointer functionality does not exist in the Adobe Connect software. Refer to Chapter 2, "Key Features of a Virtual Classroom," and especially Table 2-4 for ideas on how to use different features to accomplish the same activity.

TIP

Common Trap: Just because your virtual classroom tool allows you to include a large audience doesn't mean that you should. It's more difficult to engage and interact with a large audience, so save large audiences for events where you give a presentation and keep class sizes smaller for training events.

Blended Learning

Virtual classroom training is often part of a blended program that is incorporated into a learning program with other in-person events or technology-based activities. In such a situation, the virtual classroom may be used as a kick-off session followed by an in-person event or series of events. It may also be included as a follow-up session offered days or weeks after a traditional classroom event. Virtual classroom training is often blended with self-paced e-learning and offered as prework or postwork to the individual learning event. Refer to the examples at the end of this chapter to read different approaches for incorporating virtual classroom training into blended learning programs.

Duration

The duration of a virtual classroom session depends on the learning objectives. A good rule of thumb, however, is to segment content into 60- to 90-minute chunks. Try to give participants a break every 45 to 60 minutes, just as you would for in-person training.

Create an overall plan to help visualize the flow of the session and the length of each activity. To achieve this, use tools such as those given in Table 5-1, "Sample Session Planner Tool."

Evaluation

Your evaluation strategy is built into the design using learning objectives as a starting point. First, determine how you will monitor and evaluate progress against these objectives and what indicators you'll use to track them. Typically, the evaluation methodology is the same as classroom training, using Kirkpatrick's Four-Level Evaluation model developed by Donald Kirkpatrick. Table 5-2 describes the model and how to gather input for virtual classroom training. Levels 1, 2, and 3 require adjustment for virtual classroom training, but measuring level 4 for the virtual classroom is the same as traditional classroom training.

Adapting Face-to-Face Content

Instructional designers often adapt existing classroom content for delivery through a virtual classroom. Since this is a common practice, follow these steps to ensure the process goes smoothly and produces effective training. Refer to Appendix E, "Example of Course Conversion," for an example of a course that was converted from face-to-face to virtual classroom delivery.

Table 5-1 Sample Session Planner Tool

Time (in minutes)	Objectives	Topics	Activity or Learning Methods	Support Materials
5	Opening and introductions	• Welcome • Overview of course • Introductions • Interaction warm-up	• Discussion • Group warm up exercises (poll, chat, instant feedback)	• Slides
5	Identify types of reports	• What reports do • Four types of reports • Describe four types	• Discussion • Application sharing	• Test application • Sample reports
20	Select the right report	• Tips for selecting the right report • Consider reports you already send/receive • Ingredient list	• Discussion • Group exercise (ingredient list)	• Whiteboard
10	Run, export, save report	• Steps to run standard reports • Steps to save standard reports • Steps to export reports • Export options	• Demonstration • Discussion • Individual exercise	• Test application • Sample reports
5	Best practices, tips, and resources	• Best practices and tips: Accessing the best practices site • Resources available: Report list, reports manual	• Discussion • Demonstration	• Best practices site • Test application • Reports manual
5	Answer questions and conduct review activity	• Review main points • Answer questions	• Discussion	• Whiteboard
5	Closing/ summary	• Review • Evaluation	• Discussion	• Evaluation link
55 Minutes Total				

Adapted from Corbett, Wendy Gates and Cindy Huggett. "Designing for the Virtual Classroom." *ASTD Infoline*, Alexandria, VA: ASTD Press, 2009.

Table 5-2 The Kirkpatrick Four-Level Evaluation Model Applied to Virtual Classroom Training

Level	Method
1. **Reaction:** How well did the learners like the learning program?	• Use the feedback tool available in your virtual classroom tool, or • Send an online evaluation to participants to complete at the end of a session or after the session ends.
2. **Learning:** What did participants learn?	• Conduct an online pretest and posttest and measure knowledge change.
3. **Behavior:** To what extent did the learner's behavior change?	• Interview mangers, participants or subordinates after a time gap has occurred to determine how job performance/behavior has changed. • Conduct an online evaluation with managers, participants or subordinates after a time gap has occurred to determine how job performance/behavior has changed.
4. **Results:** What are the effects on the business or environment resulting from the learner's performance (e.g., reduced cost, improved quality, increased production, reduced turnover)?	• Analyze data from existing management systems and establish correlation to the learning program.

Step 1: Course Inventory

Start by conducting a course inventory and review all materials that relate to the course including handouts, workbooks, facilitator guide, and marketing materials. While you won't use all of these materials for your virtual classroom session, you may be able to repurpose much of the content.

Step 2: Develop a Sequence of Events

Plan to use your time judiciously. Review your learning objectives and your materials to decide what must be covered in the live session and what content can be assigned as individual prework or postwork (such as introductory information or supplemental information that falls in the "nice-to-have" category). Focus your time in the virtual classroom on interactive discussions and collaborative work using your Session Planner Tool (Table 5-1).

INVENTORY OF MATERIALS

If you are converting an in-person course to a virtual session, you already have a wealth of materials that will serve as a starting point. Your list may include:

- ✓ Prerequisite reading
- ✓ Slides
- ✓ Posters
- ✓ Handouts
- ✓ Job aids
- ✓ Workbooks
- ✓ Exercises/exercise answer sheets
- ✓ Course website
- ✓ Course discussion board/forum
- ✓ Facilitator guide
- ✓ Course timeline
- ✓ Administrator guide
- ✓ Videos
- ✓ Marketing materials (course description, target audience)
- ✓ Email messages
- ✓ Postcourse materials
- ✓ Postcourse evaluation

Prework

Well-designed prework, such as reading or exercises, helps to equalize the knowledge level for the audience. It also lets you maximize the time you have for presenting content that needs to be covered in real time.

For example, if you already have a self-paced e-learning module with introductory content, then completing this module can be used as a prerequisite to participation in the virtual classroom training. If the e-learning module is hosted in your organization's learning management system, you can track and monitor completion rates. You might even convert some of this existing introductory content into a prereading assignment and ask participants to complete a precourse knowledge test to confirm their understanding of the material, to assess skills gaps, or to gather opinions and ideas.

No matter how you decide to design prework, make sure that the instructions are clear, the participants have ample time to complete the assignment(s), and the prework is explicitly linked to the live virtual classroom training.

Postwork

A postwork assignment gives participants the opportunity to practice the knowledge and skills they gained during the virtual training event. For example, you might develop a worksheet with a list of scenarios participants may encounter in the workplace and provide a section for participants to capture notes about how they handled each encounter using the new skills learned during the virtual classroom session.

Step 3: Adjust Content and Exercises

Simply taking materials designed for in-person training, posting them in a virtual classroom tool, and expecting a successful training session result is a recipe for disaster. Exercises designed for use by a classroom facilitator must be adjusted for use on a computer screen. This can be done by utilizing all the available features in your virtual classroom tool. Table 5-3 includes ideas on how to adjust exercises. For example, if you conduct oral quizzes in the traditional classroom, it's simple to convert quiz questions to multiple-choice or

Table 5-3 Adjusting Exercises from Face-to-Face Training to the Virtual Classroom

If you do this in your face-to face training:	Try this in the virtual classroom:
Verbal quizzes	Polls
Small group work	Small group work in breakout rooms
Raising hands	Instant feedback
Writing on flip chart or whiteboard	Digital whiteboarding
Open-ended questions	Chat

true-or-false poll questions. Small group work can be transitioned to breakout rooms (provided this featured is part of your tool). And participants can "raise their hands" using the instant feedback feature. Virtual whiteboarding is no different from traditional classrooms. Use the digital whiteboard to brainstorm or summarize verbal comments or illustrate a concept. Finally, use the chat area to solicit responses to open-ended questions.

More ideas on virtual classroom exercises using the features in the virtual classroom tool are explored later in this chapter.

DEVELOPING MATERIALS

Think holistically as you develop the materials for an online virtual training session. Your list should include:

- Presentation slides
- Videos
- Exercises and interaction
- Participant workbooks
- Facilitator guide

Presentation Slides

A virtual classroom needs well-designed slides to serve as a backdrop for the course content. Chapter 4, "The Virtual Classroom Team and the Members' Roles," underscores the importance of having an instructional designer on your team with multimedia and design skills. One aspect of this person's role is to develop clear, readable slides that flow logically and enhance key messages.

In *Clear and to the Point,* author Stephen Kosslyn describes eight psychological principles for compelling PowerPoint presentations that are outlined in Table 5-4. His principles are completely transferable to designing slides for the virtual classroom. A common mistake is to put too much text on a slide. Put

Table 5-4 Eight Psychological Principles for Compelling
PowerPoint Presentations

Goal	Principle	Definition	Example
Connect with Your Audience	1. Principle of Relevance	Communication is most effective when neither too much nor too little information is presented.	If you are talking about a general difference between Japanese and U.S. consumers, don't break the information down by gender or region.
	2. Principle of Appropriate Knowledge	Communication requires prior knowledge of pertinent concepts, jargon and symbols.	If you are talking about the economics of oil production to your local Kiwanis group, link the abstract ideas to facets of everyday life, such as the price of gas, fresh produce, and even various types of synthetic clothing.
Direct and Hold Attention	3. Principle of Salience	Attention is drawn to large perceptible differences.	To make the title of a slide the most salient, make it larger and bolder that the other text. Similarly, to highlight the most important bar in a graph, color it brighter than the others.
	4. Principle of Discriminability	Two properties must differ by a large enough proportion or they will not be distinguished.	Consider those fancy and elaborate backgrounds that the PowerPoint program so conveniently provides, which range from cosmic scenes to complex geometric patterns. The backgrounds can make reading text the visual equivalent of sorting wheat from chaff, and can turn your slide into a puzzle to be solved.
	5. Principle of Perceptual Organization	People automatically group elements into units, which they then attend to and remember.	Labels should be closer to the object (or, in a graph, to the wedge, line, or bar) that they label than to anything else.

the content details in the participant workbook, job aid, or other handouts and not in the slides. Graphs and tables should be labeled appropriately with only the most relevant details that are easily seen. Fonts and color options should be used for a purpose such as highlighting differences between data points or helping participants make connections.

Table 5-4

Goal	Principle	Definition	Example
Promote Understanding and Memory	6. Principle of Compatibility	A message is easiest to understand if its form is compatible with its meaning.	A vivid illustration of this principle was provided by John Ridley Stroop in 1935. Stroop showed people the names of colors written in various colors of ink. For example, the word "red" was written in red, blue, or green ink. When participants were asked to report the color of the ink (not to read the word), they took more time and made more errors when the word named a color different from the color of the ink than when the word named a color the same color of the ink.
	7. Principle of Informative Changes	People expect changes in properties to carry information.	If part of a graph is a projection to the future, it should look different (perhaps darker or over a colored screen) from the part that summarizes the actual data.
	8. Principle of Capacity Limitations	People have a limited capacity to retain and process information, and so will not understand a message if too much information must be retained or processed.	Showing all 64 boxes in a complex organizational chart will overwhelm the audience. But the audience can absorb this information if you build up the slide a portion at a time. For instance, you can present the top layers (where proximity will group them first), and then show successive lower layers on the slide (graying out the upper layers, to direct attention to the new material—but keeping the grayed-out portions just barely discriminable in order to preserve the overall context).

Reprinted by permission of Oxford University Press, USA, from *Clear and to the Point: 8 Psychological Principles for Compelling PowerPoint Presentations* by Kosslyn (2007) 526w from pages 4–11.

Presentation Flow

It is a good idea to keep slides moving in the virtual classroom and not linger on a slide more than two or three minutes, since virtual classroom participants can't see the facilitator gesturing, pointing, and using other techniques to keep the audience's attention. Unless participants are actively engaged in an exercise, such as answering a poll, typing in text chat, or discussing a topic, it's best to cover only one key concept per slide. This will result in more slides, but the amount of content won't change. Adding appropriate graphics and images also helps encapsulate and convey key concepts. Keep in mind that adding more slides does not mean that you need to increase the pace of your delivery.

Here's an example. Imagine you are teaching a course on evaluation of workplace learning, and your workbook contains a page on Kirkpatrick's Four-Level Evaluation model. You plan to provide a three-minute introduction. The slide from a face-to-face training might contain the following text:

Level 1: Reaction—I liked it.
Level 2: Learning—I learned something.
Level 3: Behavior—I did something different.
Level 4: Results—The training had direct business impact.

However, the main content area must be more dynamic, since you, the dynamic facilitator, are not visible. If you plan to spend a few minutes on a concept, make sure that the screen does not remain static and unchanging. For example, in the four levels example above, you might turn this section into five slides: one introductory slide plus four slides for each of the four levels as

---

TIP

Recall a well-produced news segment where you saw an interview interspersed with screen visuals and think how you can apply these techniques in your session design.

shown in Figure 5-1. Details of the four levels of evaluation would be covered in the participant workbook, so they are not needed on the slide.

Spreading the content over more slides and not increasing the amount of content keeps the screen moving naturally. And by adding an image that supports the slide's concept, visual learners are supported.

Images

Images not only make slides more visually appealing, they help participants understand and retain key concepts. Garr Reynolds, author of *Presentation Zen,* says that images are more powerful and more efficient than words and that we need to look at presentations differently. His advice is to review your slides and ask what words can be replaced with an image or graphic.

Once you've located images to represent key concepts and ideas, follow these tips (for PowerPoint 2010 and 2013) to enhance them to make the images look professional.

Figure 5-1 Kirkpatrick's Four-Level Evaluation model.

1. **Outline images:** Give your images a polished look by applying a "picture style." In PowerPoint click on the image to reveal the Picture Tools feature activated at the top of the screen. Then select an appealing picture style.

2. **Remove the background from an image:** It's easy to remove an image background to make it blend in better with a slide. Just click on the image to activate the PowerPoint Picture Tools feature and select Remove Background.

3. **Incorporate text onto images:** One way to create appealing and professional images is to select an image with enough blank space to add text.

For example, if you had an image of a blank sign post, you could easily customize it for your specific requirements. Just click Insert on the PowerPoint menu bar, select the Text Box option, draw a text box on the image, and resize it to fit. Now customize the image as you wish by including text and color.

Find images for your slides on the following.

Paid sites:
- Dreamstime.com
- Fotolia.com
- Istockphoto.com
- Thinkstockphotos.com

Free site:
- Flickr.com/creativecommons

Adding Slides

Slides help you communicate clearly with participants. If the training has already been delivered in person, then start with the slide deck from the in-person training. Key slides to consider adding that are unique to virtual classroom training include the following types.

- **Facilitator Slide**: Photos, names, titles, and locations of the facilitation team.
- **Participant Slide**: Photos, names, titles, and locations of participants.
- **Interactive Features Slide**: Instructions on how to interact using the features of the virtual classroom (e.g., chat, raise hand, whiteboard tools) with a screen shot of the feature.
- **Audio Slide**: Description of how audio works (one-way or two-way audio, how teleconference works, etc.).
- **Agenda Slide**: Show the order of topics and break times. Insert this slide throughout your training between sections as you conclude a topic and start a new one.

- **Materials Slide**: If you sent materials to participants prior to the session, show a photo of the materials and describe what materials participants need and how they will be used. An example is a picture of the workbook and laminated job aid that will be used in the session.
- **Exercise Instruction Slides**: For each exercise, create a slide with clear instructions that describes the exercise, how long it will last, which interactive features will be used, and any materials needed to complete the exercise.
- **Transition Slide**: Slide that signals the transition to a new topic or new facilitator.
- **Break Slide**: Slide indicating that the class is on a break and what time the break ends.

TIP

Every time you display something on your slides that corresponds to a page in the participant handbook, show that page number on the slide. Develop a uniform way to display the page number and point out what this means to participants the first time it appears.

Video Files

Playing video in a virtual classroom is a great way to add variety to your instruction. Since video takes up a large amount of bandwidth, use it in small 1- to 2-minute segments and always display video originating from your meeting room rather than streaming it live from the web. If you plan to use a video from YouTube, try using a tool like YouTube Downloader to convert the video into a file that you can upload to your classroom. If you did not develop the video, ensure you have permission from the owner before using it.

Test your video with another person to see how it works before using it with an audience. If you are using VoIP for your session, the video file provides the audio directly through the participant computer speakers or headset. If a conference call is running simultaneously with the virtual classroom, test the video to make sure this configuration works.

Exercises and Interaction Using the Features of the Virtual Classroom

Keeping the audience engaged is vital to a successful virtual class, so well-planned exercises that offer sufficient interactivity are essential. Fortunately, most virtual classroom tools provide help to ease the transition from face-to-face to online training—all it takes is a little creativity.

Using the Chat Feature

The chat feature offers a simple way to interact with participants and requires minimal preparation. Chat can be used to welcome and warm up participants, engage participants with specific parts of your material, and simply serve as a place for participants to ask questions and share comments.

Chat Introductions

A common use of the chat feature is to acknowledge participants when they enter the room by typing a quick hello or welcome. Beyond an initial welcome, chat can be used to conduct introductions by asking participants to type their role or location and what they hope to learn from the session. While a verbal introduction like this takes up precious time in a virtual classroom, conducting introductions via the chat feature takes only seconds. Quick icebreakers, such as asking participants to type their favorite food or dream vacation ideas, are other easy ways to get participants engaged right away and familiarize them with the chat feature. See Chapter 9, "Ideas for Icebreakers and Exercises." Chapter 6, "Facilitation Techniques," covers specific techniques to use when you work with the chat feature.

Content-Based Chat Exercises

The chat feature can also be woven into the main content of your session. For example, use chat to challenge participants to think about a topic and how it applies to their situation. If the topic is stakeholder analysis, ask participants to name their key stakeholders in the chat box. When you ask this question, show a slide with the question, along with instructions that explain these directions to the participants.

The chat feature can also be used for small group work. For example, assign participants a chat partner to discuss a topic. To conduct an exercise like this, show a slide with the names of the chat pairs, instructions on how to conduct a private chat, the topic to discuss, and chat duration.

Tools, such as Adobe Connect, allow for multiple, simultaneous chat pods (pods are the panels that make up the layout for your classroom in Adobe Connect) on the screen. A fun and interactive way to use multiple chat pods is to show one chat pod in which participants type "advantages" and another chat pod for "disadvantages." Ask participants to type in both chat areas to get a conversation going and comment on the responses. See Figure 5-2 for an example of this exercise.

What are the **advantages** and **disadvantages**
of virtual classroom training
(compared to face-to-face classroom training)?

ADVANTAGES (Everyone)	DISADVANTAGES (Everyone)
Ryan White: Reach people in multiple time zones	**Maria Lee:** Participants may not be comfortable with technology
Jill Lowe: convenienient	**Samatha Williams:** Difficult to know who is paying attention
Ryan White: global reach	**Ryan White:** Facilitators have to be retrained
Samatha Williams: more cost effective	**Ryan White:** There is a perception that virtual classroom training is not as good as face to face training
Samatha Williams: interactive features	**Samatha Williams:** technical challenges
Gerome Dallas: easy to connect people in different locations	**Gerome Dallas:** You can only do short segments of training - you can't have someone attend virtual training all day
Samatha Williams: It's environmentally friendly	**Samatha Williams:** Gerome, isn't this an advantage as well? People learn better when information is shared in short segments.
Maria Lee: Less expensive than face to face training	**Gerome Dallas:** Yes, good point Samantha. It's good for the learners and it's more work for the learning teams
Jill Lowe: Virtual classroom training is less disruptive than face to face training since you attend from your office or desk	
Dmitri Hort: Very convenient and easy to participate in virtual training, like this one!	
Gerome Dallas: Interactive features make it easy to connect with participants	

Figure 5-2 Adobe Connect multiple, simultaneous chat pods.

POLLING TIPS

1. Write concise poll questions and responses.
2. Avoid acronyms and unclear language.
3. Avoid double-barreled questions.
4. Avoid leading or biased questions.
5. Use answer sets that are mutually exclusive.
6. Answer sets with numbers should be in equal increments.
7. Include a don't know or not applicable (N/A) option when appropriate.

Using Polls

Polls are simple to create and incorporate into your content. However, polling should never be done for the sake of polling; it should be done with a specific purpose in mind. For example, polling may be done to gain audience information, to quiz participants, to allow participants to self-reflect, or to evaluate your session in real time.

Writing polls and determining how to integrate them is an iterative process that happens as you develop an online session. When you see an opportunity for a poll, add a place holder slide for the poll to "bookmark" the spot and continue with the development of the session content. Then write the polls as the content is finalized. If you develop polls in this manner, you'll avoid including too many polls or polls that are unwarranted.

Writing Poll Questions and Responses

One way to think about polls in a virtual classroom is to consider them mini-surveys. A poll has two main parts: (1) the question or comment line and (2) the responses.

Best practices for formulating questions include:

■ **Keep it short:** Keep the question clear and concise, and use plain language. Review each word of the question to make sure it's necessary, simplifying any unclear language. An example of a wordy question is: "If given a choice of taking a self-directed course or an instructor-led course to learn about corporate governance, which would you prefer?" This question can be reworded and shortened but still maintain the essence of the question: "Do you prefer a self-directed or instructor-led course to learn about corporate governance?"

■ **Avoid double-barreled questions:** A double-barreled question contains two issues or ideas. For example: "How often do you search for and enroll in classes using the learning management system?" A person who searches for classes on a regular basis but never enrolls would have difficulty answering this question. If they did, the validity of the poll results would be questionable. Breaking this question into two questions solves the problem: "How often do you search for classes using the learning management system?" and "How often do you enroll in classes using the learning management system?"

■ **Eliminate acronyms and unclear language:** Avoid acronyms or spell them out in the question. For example: "How often do you use the new LMS?" Don't assume that your participants know what LMS stands for—spell out "Learning Management System." A clear way to write this question is, "How often do you use the new learning management system (LMS)?"

■ **Avoid leading or biased questions:** A leading question prompts the participants to respond in a particular way. For example, "Why do you prefer an e-learning course for further training on project management?," assumes that the respondent prefers e-learning. Rewording this question to "Which of the following delivery modes do you prefer for receiving further training on project management?" eliminates the bias of the question.

Best practices for formulating responses include:

■ **Use plain language and limit answer choices:** Similar to poll qustions, use plain and simple language. Keep the responses short and limit the number of possible responses to prevent overwhelming participants with choices. This allows an audience to quickly scan the list and locate their choice.

■ **Use mutually exclusive responses:** The list of responses also needs to be mutually exclusive for a multiple choice question. For example, if you ask the participants where they are right now, and the choice of responses is "At work, at home, at a hotel," how would someone respond who is working in a home office? Also, carefully review your responses with number ranges to make sure that the ranges don't overlap. If a person had been at an organization for three years, how would he or she choose from these responses: "0–3 years, 3–6 years"? For both of these examples, the overlap in the responses needs to be eliminated.

■ **Use number increments in equal amounts:** Check for balance in number range responses. For example, if you ask participants how much time they might devote to an e-learning course on corporate governance, the responses could be in 20-minute increments: "Less than 20 minutes, 21–40 minutes, 41–60 minutes, More than 60 minutes."

■ **Include options for outliers:** The range of responses needs to include an option for anyone who may be an "outlier." An outlier is someone whose response varies greatly from the rest of the group. Review your responses, and make sure that you offer answer choices for everyone, not just those with the most common experiences. Common outlier responses include "Other," "Not applicable," or "None of the above."

■ **Include a "Don't Know" option if appropriate:** Include a "don't know" option for questions that not every participant may be able to answer. Offering a "don't know" option allows the entire audience to respond to the poll. If you have 20 participants, it is best to see 20 responses to a poll. Anything less might mean an unengaged participant.

Types of Polls

Polls can be used in a variety of ways throughout your session including introductory polls to find out about participants, content-based polls to get participants to connect with your content, and concluding polls to see what participants learned or their feedback on the session.

■ **Introductory Polls:** Introductory polls serve the dual purpose of warming up the audience and getting them used to the polling feature. Determine what would be interesting to know about participants or for participants to know about each other before the main content of the session is presented. For example, an opening poll might ask: "Where are you located?" or "How many years have you worked for the ABC Company?" Responses to these types of polls provide essential information to the facilitation team about the background of participants that help guide the session. Polls can be used as icebreakers as well—see Chapter 9, "Ideas for Icebreakers and Exercises," for specifics.

■ **Content-Based Polls:** Once training is underway, you can use different types of polls that relate directly to the learning objectives and content of the session. You might choose to lead off each section of content with a poll to gauge the audience's knowledge of a topic. For example: "How many years have you been doing data analysis?" If you plan to share statistics or data, an interesting way to stimulate the audience is to pose questions about the data prior to revealing the data. For example, here's a sample poll question covering a data point: "What percent of accredited universities in the United States offer online degrees?" After the audience responds, display the poll results juxtaposed against the actual data on a slide. Integrating polls into the main content of the session using these techniques will maintain the attention and pique the interest of the audience.

■ **Concluding Polls:** As your session concludes, you may post polls to quiz the audience on what was covered or post a few final polls to gather feedback on the session. Using quiz questions at the end of the session is a good way to highlight key points you want participants to remember from the training. Some virtual classroom tools offer a quiz feature that can also be incorporated into your session.

Putting time and thought into polling questions and thinking about how you will utilize them during a session will help you maximize the polling feature's value.

Using Breakout Rooms

Imagine that the facilitator at an in-person classroom with tables of 5 to 6 participants asks each group to discuss a topic. The breakout room in a virtual classroom serves a similar purpose. When you want participants to work in small groups, use the breakout room feature to divide participants into small groups. Participants in a breakout room can brainstorm, design, prioritize, or debate, just like in the physical classroom.

A breakout room exercise requires clear instructions, including a time limit and defined expectations about group output. For example, if you want participants to spend 15 minutes in a breakout room discussing time management techniques, give them written and verbal instructions such as: "We are going to do a 15-minute exercise on time management techniques in breakout rooms. Each breakout room has five participants. The group names and leaders are listed here and posted in each room as well. Your objective is to brainstorm time management techniques as a group and write your top five tips on the whiteboard in your room."

Moving participants into and out of breakout rooms requires practice and patience, so use breakout rooms when you need deep interactive discussion. If the discussion won't last more than 10 minutes, just keep participants in the main virtual room and have a plenary discussion.

Audio in the Breakout Room

Unlike the other features described in this chapter, the breakout room is closely intertwined with the audio feature. Your choice of audio (VoIP or teleconference) will determine how the audio works in the breakout rooms. If all participants are using integrated two-way VoIP or integrated conference call, then the audio feature will "follow" participants into the breakout rooms.

However if you are using a conference call that is not integrated into the virtual classroom, the breakout room audio must be handled manually. For example, you can set up unique teleconference lines for each breakout room and have participants hang up and call the break out room conference call number. When the breakout room work is complete, participants simply hang up and call the main classroom number again. This method requires extra time and participants must be thoroughly briefed on how to switch teleconference lines, so use it judiciously.

Using the Whiteboard

The whiteboard allows the facilitator and participants to write and draw in a common space and can be used in a variety of ways to interact with participants.

PRESESSION SLIDE SHOW

Just as movie theaters entertain audiences before the show begins, savvy facilitators use the time before the training session begins by posting a presession slide show. The content of the slides should be informative and entertaining, but should also support the material covered in your course. Consider including the following in the presession slide show.

- Interesting statistics: For example, a computer security course might include a statistic about the number of attempted computer hacks.
- Famous quotations that relate to your topic: A writing course might include a quotation from Mark Twain or Shakespeare.
- Quiz question followed by the answer: Show a photo of a person or place and ask a simple multiple-choice question before showing the answer.
- Logistical information: Remind participants about materials they need to have ready, where they can find materials for download, start/end time, and other frequently asked questions (FAQs).
- Marketing information: Remind participants about upcoming courses, follow-up seminars, etc.

Each minute of a virtual classroom is precious, so make the most of the lead time with a presession slide show that piques the interest of participants and gets them into a learning mindset. Who knows, you may find a presession slide show so helpful that you include it in your face-to-face trainings as well.

For a warm-up exercise with a group of geographically dispersed participants, draw a map and ask people to indicate their name on the map based on their location. Or, ask a question and ask participants to draw a picture that represents a concept you are discussing. Drawing on a whiteboard will not result in a sophisticated image and the results are sometimes amusing because most people have difficulty drawing, but the fun of the exercise can also build engagement and connection.

If drawing on a whiteboard isn't a good match for your subject matter or participants' learning styles, consider using a combination of the pointer tools and the whiteboard or the pointer tools and a background slide. For example, if your session is about presentation skills, show a slide with images of a mouth, an ear, and a pair of eyes. Ask participants to point to the image that represents the most important aspect of public speaking; then select a few people to explain their choice.

The whiteboard can also be used in conjunction with a breakout room. Ask each breakout room group to draw a picture of a scenario or a process. At the conclusion of the exercise, bring the whiteboards into the main room so everyone sees the results, and ask the team leader from each breakout room to describe the group's drawing.

Participant Workbooks

Just as in face-to-face training, participants also need support materials for the virtual classroom. Create a detailed handbook for participants that, in addition to course content, contains instructions for pre- and postsession activities. If you already have a participant handbook for your traditional training, use it as a starting point and make necessary adjustments for the virtual classroom.

Since virtual classroom participants need slightly different information than in-person participants, consider adding information, such as how to access the virtual classroom, start and end times, and a link to a time zone convertor in the introduction. In addition, let participants know whom to contact if they experience technical difficulties and provide a list of FAQs that explains how to resolve common technical issues.

Facilitator Guide

The facilitator guide is a written set of instructions describing the sections of a training session, what will be covered in each section, and the content covered on each slide, accompanied by a description (or image) of the participant's view when the facilitator is speaking. It also describes how the features of the virtual classroom will be used to execute exercises and interactivity. A timeline is built into the script to ensure that the material is covered in the time allotted for the session. See Table 5-5 for a sample section of a facilitator guide. Note the detail required to orchestrate the interactivity.

Facilitator guides differ based on the needs of the facilitation teams. Some facilitators may use the notes section of PowerPoint to add information about the duration of the slide and related interactivity that will take place while the slide is displayed. No matter what format you use, it is important to have documentation noting roles and responsibilities during the virtual classroom and the length of each section.

Table 5-5 Sample Facilitator Guide

Topic: Writing Concisely					
Running Time	Duration	Slide	Facilitator	Producer	Notes
9:30	5 minutes	Introduction slide: Compare two paragraphs.	Tell participants to turn to page 5 and read the two versions of the paragraph silently. After two minutes, ask participants to respond to the poll.	Post poll: "Which version do you prefer?"	Broadcast poll results after all participants have answered.
9:35	10 minutes	Slide with the two paragraphs from the participant workbook page 5.	Call on a participant to comment on the paragraph she selected. Lead a verbal discussion about the differences. Use writing tool to cross through unnecessary words in paragraph A.	Monitor chat.	
9:45	5 minutes	Slide with tips on writing concisely.	Review bullets on slide and summarize.	Monitor chat.	

> **TIP**
>
> **Michelle Hall, eLearning & Multimedia Team Lead at the U.S. Department of Energy National Training Center**
>
> Our virtual classroom training is much more scripted than our in-person training. It's important that virtual classroom training stay on track, and the scripting also helps the facilitator and producer work together. Our facilitator guides have three columns: One for what the participant sees on the screen, one for what the facilitator says, and one for what actions the producer takes.

LEARNING AND PERSONALITY STYLES

People have different learning preferences: seeing (visual), hearing (auditory), and doing (kinesthetic). Some people tend to favor one style of learning over another, while others combine of two or more of these learning styles.

- **Visual:** Prefers learning through seeing images, graphs, video, and demonstrations.
- **Auditory:** Prefers learning through listening to instructions and audio recordings.
- **Kinesthetic:** Prefers learning through hands-on activities, moving, participating in simulations, and physical activities. Likes to solve problems by physically working them through.

Furthermore, participants usually include a mix of introverts and extroverts who process and think about information differently. In general, introverts need time to process information silently by themselves, while extroverts prefer to talk aloud as they process information.

Since all virtual classrooms will contain participants with a variety of preferences, it's important to develop activities that will engage all learning styles. Table 5-6 provides examples of activities which cater to different learning and personality styles.

Table 5-6 Learning and Personality Styles

Learning Style	Sample Activities
Visual	• Show an image of a flow chart while you describe it. • Display specific instructions for an activity before starting the activity.
Auditory	• Give a mini-lecture of five minutes followed by an independent exercise. • Participate in small and large group discussions before working independently.
Kinesthetic	• Use the whiteboard to conduct an activity and ask participants to draw or write a response.
Personality Style	**Sample Activities**
Introvert	• Show a slide with a question and give participants 1–2 minutes to write their responses in their workbook. Repeat this one or two times, and then ask participants to reflect on their response and select an observation to share with the class.
Extrovert	• Show a slide with a question and ask participants to brainstorm aloud possible solutions.

TIP

Stephanie Zaitsev, Organization Development Consultant/Trainer from Training Resources Group

Virtual classroom design mirrors face-to-face classroom design. It's important to have a good balance of visuals and graphics and make sure that what you are saying matches what participants are seeing. Just like in the face-to-face classroom, we make sure that the design of exercises caters to both introverts and extroverts. For example, in face-to-face training we ask participants to think about an example and write it down before sharing with the class in order to give introverts time to process their thoughts. In virtual classroom training we do the same thing, although we may have them type a response in chat instead of responding verbally.

GAMIFICATION IN THE VIRTUAL CLASSROOM

Gamification, the process of applying gaming designs and concepts to learning or training scenarios, is an important and growing technique used to engage participants and make learning fun. In the virtual classroom, it is still in the early stages of development, but gamification is rapidly becoming mainstream elsewhere.

INTERVIEW WITH KARL KAPP, PROFESSOR OF INSTRUCTIONAL TECHNOLOGY, BLOOMSBURG UNIVERSITY

Gamification in the virtual classroom is still in its infancy. Currently, instructors use workarounds to apply gamification techniques since the technology does not yet support the introduction of game-like elements into the virtual classroom. For example, we run an exercise in the virtual classroom that allows students to write an answer in a grid on the whiteboard. When all the answers are posted, each student gets to rank the answers by writing numbers for responses that he or she considers the best. Students with the highest number of #1 ranking responses win the game. The gamification elements in this type of exercise are points, ranking, social relatedness, immediate feedback, and sense of community.

Another technique that virtual classroom instructional designers can apply is to let participants have some influence on the direction of the action in the classroom in real time, just like we do when we play a game. For example, a designer creates a set of PowerPoint slides that tell a story, loaded with images and a character that appears throughout the slide deck. The slide deck contains content divided by sections based on what "path" the character takes. When the character has to make a choice, the facilitator posts a poll and based on the tallied poll results, the facilitator jumps to the corresponding slide section.

For example, in a class on leadership, a character on the slide might be confronted with three options for resolving an ethical dilemma. The instructor asks the students to choose from among the options via a poll. The results of the poll dictate which slide the instructor goes to next based on the option chosen by the option chosen by the majority of the class.

The facilitator has to be willing to give a little bit of control to participants in order for this to work. However, designing training like this encourages participation because it adds an element of unpredictability.

Gamification in the virtual classroom will continue to evolve as vendors add technical features to make it easier for participants to complete an activity and see how they did compared to other participants, display badges for earning points, and so on.

USE CASES

Envisioning training in the virtual classroom is best accomplished by reading about how others develop and conduct programs. Consider the use cases below and examples from a variety of organizations.

....

Qualcomm: Adrienne Loder, Senior Learning Specialist (Figure 5-3)

We had a 40-hour management skills program for technical engineers that had been delivered in a face-to-face classroom. As the company grew, it became difficult to deliver the course globally with consistent content quality, so we redesigned it as a blended learning program. Our offices in San Diego consist of 47 buildings distributed across seven miles, so the virtual classroom is convenient to get people together for short amounts of time, and we can also still bring people together for training in a physical classroom.

Now the course is delivered over six months, and it is a combination of virtual classroom events and in-person workshops. The virtual classroom events are two hours long on average, and participants learn a concept, see it modeled, then practice in breakout rooms. In the in-person two-day workshops, we have discussions, debates, and review a 360 leadership development report to help participants customize their development plans based on their feedback.

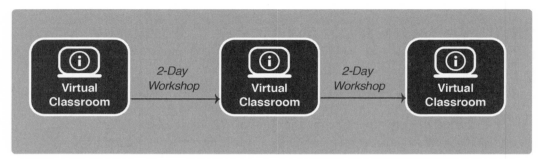

Figure 5-3 Qualcomm combines virtual classroom training with two-day workshops.

With this model, we are able to increase the delivery of the course from four offerings a year to eight without impacting the quality of the learner experience. Each cohort is made up of 30 participants. Delivering training virtually and having the managers get used to working virtually with others also has an important side effect: Many managers are not colocated with their direct reports, and the course makes them better at virtual interactions overall.

The virtual classroom sessions are very interactive. Since improving management skills isn't something you can learn through osmosis, we give participants a lot of opportunity to practice skills in breakout rooms. We have two facilitators and one producer for each session. The facilitators move from breakout room to breakout room in much the same manner as they would walk around a face-to-face classroom—making sure that no groups are "stuck." We use Adobe Connect and when we bring participants back into the main room, we bring their chat notes from the breakout room back into the main room so we can have it as a backdrop when we have plenary discussion.

The virtual classroom facilitators have to have a "tight" delivery in order to keep the pace interactive. You only get one chance to make a good first impression, so make sure you are well prepared for your virtual classroom training.

···

TD Bank: Peggy Page, Design Group Manager (Figure 5-4)

We offered a six-hour in-person course for branch managers on how to conduct behavioral interviews. Although there was a lot of interest in the course, managers were reluctant to give up a day to come to training—it just wasn't practical. So we converted the course to a virtual delivery for a class size of 11 to 12 participants.

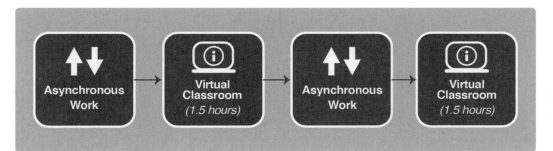

Figure 5-4 TD Bank's model combines asynchronous work with virtual classroom training.

Here's how the course works: When a manager enrolls online, he or she automatically receives an e-workbook about behavioral interviews. The e-workbook is prereading to be completed before the first virtual classroom session. The first virtual classroom session is about analyzing the job you are hiring for and crafting interview questions. Participants discuss the questions they plan to ask. After the first session, participants watch a video of a good behavioral interview and they learn about an interview model. During the second virtual classroom session participants practice interview techniques. Participants are coached on skills such as how to ask probing questions.

Our biggest lesson learned is that audiences may not be ready to participate in virtual learning because of their physical location. For example, in some of the new bank branches, we have an open office layout and very little private space. You can't put someone in a virtual classroom where customers can see the person. In addition to a private space, they need a good headset and computer. Some organizations underestimate the amount of analysis that the trainers need to do when switching from an in-person classroom to a virtual classroom. It's an important role that the training department plays to help the organization make the most of virtual classrooms.

Training Resources Group: Meredith MacDonald Ferris and Stephanie Zaitsev, Organizational Development Trainers (Figure 5-5)

We run a three-day in-person high-potential leadership program for the International Finance Corporation. We determined that follow-up refresher training was needed, but

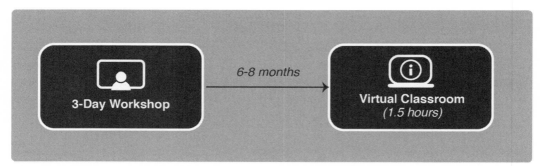

Figure 5-5 Training Resources Group model combines a three-day workshop with virtual classroom training.

doing the training in person was prohibitively expensive since the participants were in offices spread across the world. We turned to the virtual classroom since it offers a low-cost way to connect people. We created a 90-minute highly interactive leadership refresher training session for up to 10 participants. During the training, a facilitator shows a poll with key concepts taught in the course, such as open communication, giving feedback, and personal leadership. Participants are asked to pick a topic and share a success story on that topic. The poll results show the facilitators which part of the face-to-face training the participants found most applicable. The poll also serves as a launching pad to encourage participants to share experiences with their peers and engage in collaborative learning.

··

George Mason University: Shahron Williams van Rooij, PhD, Associate Professor (Figure 5-6)

I teach graduate students who are pursuing a Master of Education degree or graduate certificate in e-learning in the Instructional Design and Technology Program at George Mason University. My courses are delivered online in an asynchronous environment. Students come from a wide range of backgrounds, with different comfort levels with technology. Interestingly, my course may be the first online course a student has ever taken. At the beginning of the course, I use the virtual classroom to offer an "open mic night," which is a live session over the web where participants have the opportunity to ask questions about the course, requirements, and anything else. I explain that the open

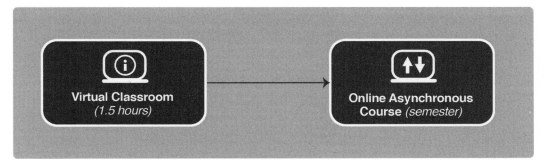

Figure 5-6 George Mason University's model combines virtual classroom training with an online asynchronous course.

mic night fulfills two main purposes: It provides a chance to ask questions, and it meets a psychological need to see the instructor. Although it's an optional session, typically all students join, and while it's not a formal training session, this creative use of gathering participants together in the virtual classroom helps form a learning connection among participants who would not otherwise get together in the physical world. I developed a simple slide deck for the session with an agenda, key points on the syllabus, and a slide to prompt participants to ask questions.

···

Habitat for Humanity: Lina Maria Obando M., Associate Director of Organizational Learning (Figure 5-7)

We offer a course for staff on how to identify and formulate project proposals to secure funding. The course formerly was delivered as a one-week workshop, but we converted it to virtual delivery and now we offer a 12-week program broken into two 6-week segments. Participants are distributed throughout Latin America, and they sign up in groups of three from various countries so they can work together in the course and on homework. We use a blended approach to deliver the course, which includes synchronous and asynchronous elements. We start with a two-hour kick-off in the virtual classroom to introduce the program and the Habitat Learn platform that participants use during the course. The asynchronous work consists of readings, videos, and exercises to help participants identify a project and start formulating a proposal. Participants are expected to complete about six hours of work per week.

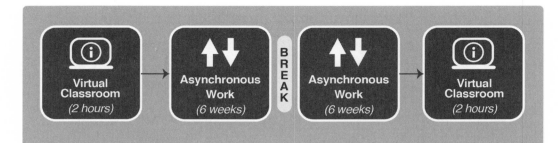

Figure 5-7 Habitat for Humanity's model starts virtual classroom training, moves to asynchronous work, and then concludes with another virtual classroom training session.

We have a one-week break in between the two sessions in part to allow participants to catch up if they need to. Throughout the six weeks of asynchronous work, participants are working with their peers and virtually with the instructor to develop their proposal. The course concludes with a virtual classroom session where participants present their proposal to a group of internal experts who are connected with funders. Not only do they get to work on presentation skills as they would in front of a committee, but also they get feedback from peers and the facilitator. When participants finish the course, they have a complete project proposal that is relevant to their work.

U.S. Department of Energy National Training Center: Michelle Hall, eLearning & Multimedia Team Lead (Figure 5-8)

We train employees at nuclear facilities around the country. During the past year, we began converting our in-person training to virtual classroom training so that we could more easily reach our target audience, whose training needs are very specialized.

For example, we offer a course on Hazard Categorization Safety that used to be a one-day in-person course. Now we deliver it as two three-hour sessions on a Tuesday and a Thursday. The course is targeted at safety analysts in nuclear facilities. It is a niche audience and we run a course with 4 to 10 participants. What's nice about the virtual classroom is that it's still cost effective to run classes with a small number of participants. If we had only four enrollees in an in-person course we would have to cancel it because it's not cost effective.

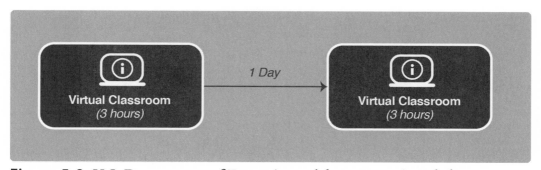

Figure 5-8 U.S. Department of Energy's model uses two virtual classroom training sessions with a one-day break.

CONTINUOUS LEARNING

1. Attend a virtual classroom training session. Analyze the content and structure of the training.
2. Write an outline of a virtual training course that you would like to develop.
3. Create your own checklist of things to look for when repurposing your training for the virtual classroom.
4. Review the materials for your virtual training and analyze the images and graphics. Do they support the key concepts of your materials? What images could you add?

References

Hastings, Nancy B. "Analysis in the Age of Distance Learning." In *2010 Pfeiffer Annual Training*, ed. Elaine Biech. San Francisco: John Wiley & Sons, 2010.

Christopher, Darlene. "Best Practices for Polling in Web Conferences." *eLearning Solutions Magazine*, October 6, 2008. Retrieved September 1, 2013, from www.elearningguild.com.

Corbett, Wendy Gates and Cindy Huggett. "Designing for the Virtual Classroom." *ASTD Infoline.* Alexandria, VA: ASTD Press, 2009.

Emerson, Tricia and Mary Stewart. *The Learning and Development Book.* Alexandria, VA: ASTD Press, 2011.

Hyder, Karen, et al. *The eLearning Guild's Handbook on Synchronous e-Learning.* Santa Rosa, CA: The eLearning Guild, 2007.

Kosslyn, Stephen Michael. *Clear and to the Point: 8 Psychological Principles for Compelling PowerPoint Presentations.* New York: Oxford University Press, 2007.

Kirkpatrick, Donald L. and James D. Kirkpatrick. *Evaluating Training Programs: The Four Levels.* San Francisco: Berrett-Koelher Publishers, Inc., 2006.

Reynolds, Garr. *Presentation Zen: Simple Ideas on Presentation Design and Delivery.* Berkeley, CA: New Riders, 2008.

Rosenberg, Marc J. *Beyond E-Learning,* San Francisco, CA: John Wiley & Sons, Inc., 2006.

SIX

Facilitation Techniques

HERE'S HOW TO:

- Facilitate sustainable interactive and engaging virtual training.
- Ensure your voice is clear and energetic.
- Use virtual classroom features to replace traditional body language cues.
- Use virtual classroom features as you facilitate.

Many of the familiar traditional facilitation techniques used in the classroom are easily transferable to the virtual classroom. Other techniques require slight adjustment. A few of the techniques in this chapter will be new to many facilitators, so expect a small learning curve on your road to proficiency. However, facilitators can quickly succeed in closing both the physical distance and skills gaps with the addition of a few new virtual techniques and by judiciously upgrading their existing facilitation skills.

Chapter 4, "The Virtual Classroom Team and the Members' Roles," explored the key skills needed to facilitate in a virtual classroom. This chapter shows you how to put these specific virtual facilitation skills into practical use to conduct interactive and engaging training that supports your learning goals.

THE SECRET TO SUSTAINED ENGAGEMENT

The secret to sustained, session-long participant engagement is early engagement. While that may seem less than profound or an unsurprising "secret" technique, it is one that really does work! Effective virtual training begins by engaging your virtual classroom audience right from the start with basic virtual tools, such as posing an interesting question in the chat area, conducting an initial poll related to the session, or launching into an entertaining exercise.

This initial engagement activity is vital for two reasons. First, this early effort really does result in a more effective learning outcome by helping you ease into more dense subject matter. Second, and perhaps more important, early and sustained virtual training engagement means a more enjoyable experience for you and your participants. Participants who have a positive disposition toward the learning experience are more likely to achieve the learning objectives of the session because they are engaged. Expecting your nonengaged learners to suddenly become engaged with the subject matter at the end of a long and content heavy session is not realistic.

Of course, most learning professionals know that lecturing to participants is not an effective training approach, so why would there be an expectation that the results would be any different in a virtual classroom? If the plan for your virtual training session consists of a 45-minute presentation followed by a 15-minute question-and-answer session, participants will quickly tune out and disengage from the training. As John Medina, author of *Brain Rules*, explains so succinctly: "Our brains don't pay attention to boring things. . . ."

Here's how to ensure that your facilitation technique is more engaging. First, actively interact with participants every three to five minutes (as noted in

> **TIP**
> Find ways to engage with participants right away. They are more likely to remain engaged throughout your session if you establish rapport early.

Chapter 5, "Developing Virtual Classroom Training," this engagement should be built right into your course design). Next, let participants know right away that you expect them to help you make the session's interactivity a two-way street. Remind them to use the virtual tools available to them, including audio, chat, and other features during the session. Here are a few techniques you can use to encourage this engagement among participants:

- Greet each participant through the chat feature or verbally as he or she enters the virtual meeting room. Explain that you and the producer will monitor the chat area throughout the session.
- Post a poll to determine how much experience each member of the audience has with the topic. Engage the audience by offering a running commentary on the number of poll responses received. Participants understand right away that you expect everyone to respond to poll questions.
- Ask participants to complete a precourse survey. Select a few interesting findings and share them on a slide. Ask for feedback from the participants in the chat area or encourage verbal responses.

TIP

Dana Peters, CEO, Mondo Learning Solutions

To prepare trainers and facilitators for the virtual classroom, we focus on the four unique connections the facilitator needs to master:

1. Connecting participants to other participants
2. Connecting participants to the content
3. Connecting the facilitator to the participants
4. Connecting the facilitator to the content

By focusing on these four areas, the facilitator learns to develop and deliver dynamic and interactive virtual classroom training that engages everyone.

These are just a few ways to encourage initial interaction with your virtual training participants. The key is to use the various virtual classroom tools to sustain participant interaction throughout the learning experience.

WORKING EFFECTIVELY WITH A PRODUCER

Partnering with an experienced producer is the best way to sustain a high level of interactivity throughout a session. The producer role is to provide a full range of virtual classroom support to the facilitator. This collaboration is most effective if you agree in advance on the specific responsibilities for each role. Sharing these classroom duties with someone else will require a period of adjustment for the facilitator, who may be accustomed to being completely in charge of the physical classroom space. With continued practice, the collaboration will improve and eventually both facilitator and producer will work together like a well-oiled machine.

TIP

Anna Heinrich, Virtual Classroom Instructional Designer, InSynch Training

Many facilitators underutilize their producers. They view the producer as technical support rather than as a training partner. The producer can track the frequency of individual participant responses and relay that information to the facilitator, who uses it to reach out to low-response participants. The producer can also help the facilitator with energy level and engagement by answering a question or making a comment if the group is too quiet. Finally, a producer can offer constructive feedback to the facilitator on how to improve during the next session.

FOCUS ON YOUR VOICE AND PACE

A facilitator's voice carries extra weight in the virtual classroom. Since participants can't rely on the facilitator's gestures or body language to pick up meaning or message nuances, the facilitator must rely on voice alone to communicate these subtleties. Here are some techniques to help a virtual facilitator to communicate more effectively with virtual learners.

Keep Your Energy Level High

Participants can sense your energy level through the tone of your voice, so their energy level and interest mirrors yours. Keep your energy level high by speaking with enthusiasm and smiling just as if you're addressing a physical classroom. Gesturing just as you would in a typical classroom setting helps maintain your own energy and enthusiasm level in your voice which keeps your virtual audience engaged.

Vary Your Voice

Truly engaged virtual classroom facilitators use a variety of volumes, pitches, and rhythms to keep their audience engaged. While these vocal techniques are important in a classroom setting, they take on special significance for virtual facilitators. Listen to various formats on the radio—talk, music, news—and compare how the announcers use their voices to convey emotions and engage their audiences, and then mimic the most appropriate styles as practice.

Eliminate Fillers and Self-Talk

Typical classroom presentation fillers such as "umms" and "ahhs" and thinking out loud to yourself, as in "now where is my pointer tool again?," may be fine in moderation before a live audience, but these devices are distracting in the virtual classroom. If you lose track of what you were saying or experience a technical glitch, your audience doesn't need to know about it. Pause for a moment to resolve the issue and continue when the issue is resolved. A skilled facilitator and experienced producer should be able to resolve these types of issues or create a backup plan without ever alerting or involving the audience.

Pause

Virtual participants need time to collect their thoughts, type responses (even more time if responding in a nonnative language), and unmute phones. Re-

---

TIP

Remember, when you ask a question participants need time to:

1. Realize that they need to respond.
2. Think of their response.
3. Take an action (type in chat, unmute phone, etc.).

Furthermore, depending on internet bandwidth and speed, a delay may occur between the time a participant types an answer and its appearance in the virtual chat box.

---

member to pause and give them time to respond when necessary. You might try counting to ten silently if a response is not immediate.

Resist the urge to jump in and break the silence even though the few seconds of "dead" airtime feels uncomfortable. If maintaining this silence is difficult even for the few appropriate seconds required, the facilitator might ask the producer to mute their phone automatically for ten seconds until they've mastered the art of pausing.

Use Clear Language

Gestures and body language often help in-person participants fill in any gaps in understanding resulting from a facilitator's use of imprecise language. Virtual facilitators, however, must pay more attention to the precision of their language to ensure that the intended information is received by the participants.

For example, if a virtual facilitator wants participants to take a specific action, such as respond to a question or turn to a page in a workbook, the facilitator must make that expectation clear. Participants can be told how to respond either by typing that request in the chat area or verbally. For example, the facilitator might say: "Kim, could you unmute your microphone and share a tip for managing stress in the workplace?" Such specificity prevents misunderstandings and participant frustration in virtual training sessions.

TIPS

Karen Hyder, coauthor of *The eLearning Guild's Handbook on Synchronous eLearning*

Online facilitators must learn to talk more because they need to give more instructions and tell participants how to respond. At the same time, facilitators have to say less if they want to keep participants engaged. For example, instead of showing a slide with a title and bullets, show a slide with a question, ask for participant input, and use the whiteboard to post comments.

The virtual facilitator must also work hard to keep the audience's attention on the screen using a variety of interactive techniques. Facilitators can test their audience attention power by watching a recording of their presentation and role playing how engaged a typical participant might react during the session.

MAKE UP FOR THE ABSENCE OF BODY LANGUAGE

Trained facilitators know that the bulk of a speaker's message is conveyed through body language, posture, and gestures, rather than the message itself. In fact, research by James Borg shows that 93 percent of communication is based on nonverbal behaviors. Most facilitators have mastered a style of classroom communication that relies on eye contact, gestures, and physical movement to get their message across. These expert facilitators are also able to gauge interest levels and understanding by reading the body language of participants. For example, a participant gazing out a window or fiddling with a pen is likely done with an exercise and a perplexed expression likely means a lack of understanding or the need to ask a question.

Most experienced classroom facilitators are acutely aware of their reliance on these visual cues in a face-to-face classroom the first time they try facilitating a virtual session. Suddenly, they are unable to "read" and interpret participant body language and react accordingly.

Fortunately the virtual classroom makes up for this deficit with a wide variety of interactive virtual engagement tools. Maximizing the use of the instant feedback feature is a great way to make up for the absence of body language. For example, ask participants to mark "agree" using the instant feedback tool if they are ready to move onto the next topic. Encourage participants to use this tool frequently throughout the session to give you feedback for example, when you need to "talk louder" or when they have "stepped away" if they need to momentarily leave the session. The type of feedback participants can provide using the instant feedback tool varies, so see what options they have and weave the use of the tool into your facilitation.

A webcam on the facilitator that allows participants to "see" the instructor can also help make up for the absence of body language to a certain extent. However, this tool comes with a number of caveats and cautions about its effectiveness.

Should you use the webcam feature for most virtual sessions? Let's explore the advantages and disadvantages of broadcasting the facilitator's face.

- **Advantage:** Participants are able to "connect" visually with the facilitator. Sometimes, just this small screen connection improves the learning experience.
- **Advantage:** You can also ask participants to turn on their webcams for just a short period of time, such as when they answer a question. Seeing other learners may help participants feel more connected.
- **Disadvantage:** Broadcasting a webcam in your virtual classroom uses valuable bandwidth. If your Internet connection speed is not sufficient to handle the increased load, the facilitator's voice and image may not sync, so that the effect is like watching a poorly dubbed movie.
- **Disadvantage:** Looking directly into the webcam is the best way to connect visually with participants. Unfortunately, that means you can't pay attention to participants interacting with you or "raising their hands" via chat or instant feedback tools. You can overcome this problem by selectively turning this video feature off and on depending on when this direct connection enhances participant engagement. For example, you might turn the video feature on for the first few minutes of a session to

establish a "social presence" with participants. Then, tell the participants that you will selectively turn this feature off and on during the session. An alternative to broadcasting yourself via webcam is to show a static photo of yourself if you wish to maintain this initial connection. You might also turn the video feature back on after a session break to indicate that the class is ready to start again.

If you do keep your webcam on throughout a session, review Appendix F, "Webcam Tips," for tips to enhance the experience for participants and help you look professional on camera.

Annotate While Speaking

Classroom facilitators typically use a laser pointer or finger to focus attention on a specific part of a slide projected onto a screen or gestures to indicate flow or direction of a process or flow chart. Most virtual classroom platforms include drawing and pointer tools, such as highlighters and writing instruments. Use these annotation tools generously to emphasize key information on the screen. For example, the facilitator might underline or circle key words on the screen during a session, point to a specific part of a graph, or draw lines or circles on the screen to indicate a graphic's direction or flow. See Figure 2-3 for an example of an annotated screen.

TIP

Debra Moore, Instructional Systems Designer, Defense Acquisition University

If you leave a slide up on the screen for too long, learners will lose focus. If you're going to leave a slide on the screen while you have a verbal discussion, have the producer add notes in real time on the screen to capture the highlights of the discussion.

Monitor Participant Feedback

Most virtual classrooms offer a variety of interactive features designed to monitor participant feedback. In live sessions, facilitators normally receive feedback from participants by observing their body language, such as nodding heads or blank stares indicating confusion. To warm up participants to use such tools, a facilitator can weave in some training on using these interactive features within the first few minutes of the session. For example, the facilitator may ask participants to answer a simple question, such as typing their location into the chat screen, or respond to a poll about their background, or indicate that the audio is working properly by "raising" their hands using the instant feedback feature. Refer to Table 6-1 for examples of how to adapt techniques used in the physical classroom to a virtual classroom.

SCAN THE ENTIRE SCREEN

New virtual facilitators have a tendency to focus only on the content or graphic that occupies the main part of the computer screen. Participants asking questions in the chat area, responding to a poll, or raising their hand may be ignored visually. Scanning multiple areas of the screen and responding appropriately while actively presenting in a session takes practice. Putting reminders in your facilitator guide to scan the screen is one easy technique to use initially as a learning tool. A skilled virtual classroom facilitator can seamlessly weave chat comments, poll results, and other participant interactions into a presentation. Eventually, an experienced virtual facilitator can gather feedback from an audience and get a sense of the "pulse" of the room with as much accuracy as most classroom facilitators.

HOW TO FACILITATE LIKE A PRO USING VIRTUAL CLASSROOM FEATURES

So what are some of the key virtual classroom features used by a facilitator and producer to effectively engage an audience and encourage learning? This sec-

Table 6-1 Traditional Classroom Facilitation Techniques Adapted to the Virtual Classroom

Traditional Classroom Facilitation	Virtual Classroom Facilitation (a producer may help with some of these techniques)
Make a comment or statement and then watch for head nods or frowns to appear to gauge agreement or disagreement.	Ask participants to use instant feedback features if they agree or disagree with a statement (Feedback features vary by system, for example: checkmark for agree, X mark for disagree, etc.).
While explaining a difficult concept, scan audience and watch for nods or quizzical looks to judge comprehension.	Tell participants to use instant feedback features to indicate if they understand and are ready to move on or not (Feedback features vary by system, for example: checkmark = move on, X mark = not ready to move on.
Watch participants to see when they look up to indicate they are done reading a document.	Tell participants to type "done" into the chat box when they have finished reading a document.
Call out a list of choices and ask each participant to raise their hand when they hear the description of their experience level with the topic to be discussed (no experience, 1–2 years, 3–4 years, etc.).	Post a poll with a question about experience level with the topic to be discussed, and ask participants to mark the response on the screen that corresponds to their experience level.
Scan the room to look for participants with a raised hand.	Scan the participant list on the screen to see if anyone has clicked the "raise hand" feature.

tion builds on what you learned in Chapter 2, "Key Features of a Virtual Classroom," about integrating available virtual classroom features into your session design.

Screen Sharing

When you activate the screen sharing feature on your virtual classroom tool, the participants may experience a screen flicker or the screen might go blank for a brief moment. Make sure you tell participants that this is normal and not a technical glitch. You might say something like: "Your screen will turn gray for a moment while I pull up the website so you can see the report."

Note that with most classroom tools, moving into screen sharing mode limits what the facilitator sees on the screen. In most cases, you'll only be able to see the website, application, or file that you are sharing. Figures 6-1 and 6-2 illustrate this effect with a comparison of the participant view and instructor view respectively.

Figure 6-1 Adobe Connect screen sharing: participant view.

Figure 6-2 Adobe Connect screen sharing: instructor view.

> # TIP
> It's a good idea to have a second computer on hand and to log in as a participant so that you can view both the instructor view and the participant view simultaneously when using the screen sharing feature. Then when you ask participants: "Do you see the website on your screens?" you'll already know the answer.

Optimize Your Screen to Avoid Distraction

Does the audience really need to see your bookmarks and other web browser personalization? Probably not, so remove all the unnecessary toolbars in your web browser to save valuable real estate on your screen and also minimize distractions. Before the session begins, test your web browser and make the appropriate changes. Figure 6-3 demonstrates the clean appearance achieved on screen by making simple browser display changes.

Figure 6-3 Adobe Connect screen sharing: participant view with toolbars removed.

Avoid Antsy Mouse Syndrome

A presenter suffering from what I call "antsy mouse syndrome" constantly moves the mouse all over the screen while using the screen sharing feature. Classroom facilitators exhibit similar distracting behavior by constantly circling

---

TIP

Use a second computer to watch your mouse movements and practice until you like what you see when you are using the screen sharing feature. Also, check if your mouse movements are visible when you click through slides that have been uploaded into the virtual classroom. Some tools allow you to hide your mouse movements when showing slides.

---

key points with a laser pointer. In either case, the action serves mainly to confuse or annoy participants.

Avoid this syndrome by making any mouse or pointer movements slow and deliberate and by giving the audience clues for the mouse or pointer's next movement. For example, the facilitator might say: "Now, I'm clicking on the Reports tab in order to open up a drop down menu. Next I'm going to select Manager Reports so that I can access individual reports." Don't use keyboard shortcuts to navigate since your participants won't be able to see these commands and movements.

Keep It Brief to Better Engage Participants

Involve the audience as much as possible when clicking through any demonstration session by asking knowledge-check questions. Keep your demonstrations brief, make a point, and then move on. Some virtual classroom tools allow the facilitator to turn over control to a participant. In these cases, allowing the participant to demonstrate learning by interacting directly with the facilitator's screen is optimal. Note that this interactive technique works best in a small class.

Practice, Practice, Practice

Practice is an essential component when using a virtual tool's screen sharing feature. Needless mouse movements and clicking through the menu bar is confusing to participants. For example, if you plan to show how to use a specific

> **TIP**
>
> If you plan to use the screen sharing feature to display a specific website, record the exact path of how you will click through to a site in the facilitator guide. Make notes to explain how to pull up the example to prevent accidentally clicking in the wrong place or, even worse, resorting to multiple clicks to find the page or example you want to show participants.

function of Excel, practice the exact sequence of steps several times, beginning with entering the screen sharing mode. Once you enter the application, click through each step deliberately as you verbally describe the process. In addition, practice how you move from screen sharing mode back into your content sharing area (where your slides are). Sometimes this requires an extra click to "stop screen sharing." Glancing at the second computer that shows the participant view can help confirm that participants are seeing what you intend them to see, whether in screen sharing mode or moving back into the main content area.

Using the Chat Feature Effectively

The chat feature allows participants and facilitators to communicate throughout a session. When the facilitator is working with a producer, the producer manages the chat area and is responsible for alerting the facilitator to any participant questions or comments. Since the facilitator is focused on managing and interacting with the virtual classroom, the producer does the majority of typing in the chat area. Here are some tips to create a successful facilitator and producer partnership with chat.

Be Deliberate with Responses

When responding to a message or comment, make sure that both the intention and recipient of a message or answer to a question is clearly identified. Here's an example of what can happen without this clarity of response. The producer responses (Kim) are bolded for emphasis.

Joe: What is the name of the advanced course?

Kim: Advanced Project Management

Maria: Is there a prerequisite for the advanced course?

Joe: Can consultants enroll too, or just employees?

Kim: no

Kim's response is not clear. Did she mean no that no prerequisite for the advanced course is required or that consultants cannot enroll? A technique for preventing this type of confusion is to practice deliberate chatting. Deliberate chatting means that you start each response with a name when needed and restate as much of the question as needed in the response. Here's the improved response.

Joe: What is the name of the advanced course?

Kim: The advanced course is Advanced Project Management

Maria: Is there a prerequisite for the advanced course?

Joe: Can consultants enroll too, or just employees?

Kim: Maria, there is no prerequisite for Advanced PM

Kim: Joe, Advanced PM is open only to employees

Responding deliberately to specific questions may take a few extra seconds of typing, but the clarity improvement is worth the effort.

TIP

Use the @ symbol before a person's name to indicate the chat message is intended for a specific person. For example @Maria, there is no prerequisite for Advanced PM.

Check Periodically for Chat Posts

When the chat area is unusually active, scroll back through the comments that have scrolled off the visible screen to see if you missed anything. If you are facilitating alone, just pause and tell the audience that you are reviewing the chat text to make sure you didn't miss any key questions or comments. If you find an important post you missed, address it either verbally or in the chat area. Your careful attention to ensuring your timely response to chat messages encourages greater participant engagement and even more lively chat interaction. If you notice that participants are helping each other in the chat area, take time to acknowledge this positive collaboration.

Say It and Type It for Maximum Clarity

Type any verbally posed questions in the chat area to ensure that participants understand your intention. This dual approach works best when a facilitator and producer work together. For example, the facilitator poses the question while the producer simultaneously types the question into the chat area. Be clear about how you want participants to respond—via chat or verbally. Note that if the participants type their responses, the facilitator should acknowledge and highlight a few good examples.

TIP

Create a text file with the questions you plan to ask participants via the chat box. When you are ready to ask the question, the producer can simply copy and paste the text into the chat box.

Weave Chat Responses into the Discussion

Weaving chat comments and questions into the verbal discussion and content delivery opens up a huge door for interactivity. When a participant asks a good question or adds an interesting comment via chat, refer to the participant(s) who posted the chat (preferably by name) in the discussion. For example: "Lee and Stan, those are both great examples of how to communicate effectively with stakeholders. Those examples remind me of what Jane noted earlier in chat about the importance of a communication plan. Let's discuss that now by turning to page 10 in your workbook. . . ."

Facilitators should not feel compelled to respond to every chat question or comment, especially if there is a large volume of posts and some are repetitive. Commenting on some of the chat posts or noting common themes you see in the chat posts is a good practice. If a participant asks a question that is off topic, you can also offer to respond individually after the class ends.

Using Public Versus Private Chat

Most virtual classroom tools have a feature that allows you to chat privately (with a single participant) or publicly (with all participants). Part of the facilitator's (or producer's) role is to decide whether a public or private response is the most appropriate response. In most cases, if a chat exchange benefits all participants, then it should be public, but if the exchange does not have widespread benefit, then a private chat is preferable. Review Table 6-2 for examples of public and private chat messages.

The quick pace of the virtual classroom can be confusing and is complicated by the fact that both the participants and facilitators can choose who receives their chat message. The producer has a responsibility to check carefully that these messages are sent and delivered to the right person.

Table 6-2 Examples of Public Versus Private Chat Messages

Public Chat Examples	Private Chat Examples
Participant posts a clarifying question or makes a comment about what is being discussed. *(That example is exactly what happened to me last week!)*	Participant joined late and needs to know what page of the workbook to turn to. *(I've just joined—can you tell me what page we are on?)*
Producer responds to participant questions and comments where the response will benefit most of the participants and not a single person. *(All of these techniques are defined in the glossary on page 25 of your workbook.)*	Participant is having a unique technical problem. *(My screen is now just a gray square where the slides were just showing. Are we supposed to be seeing slides?)*
Producer types messages to emphasize key points that the speaker is making. *(An active listener spends more time listening than speaking.)*	Participant types that he needs to step away from the session. *(I have been called into an emergency meeting. I will step away and rejoin in 15 minutes.)*
	Participant provides personal feedback such as his/her nickname or the mispronunciation of his/her name by the facilitator. *(I prefer to be called Bill.)*

Facilitators and producers can eliminate confusion by ensuring that participants understand chat etiquette. Facilitators might say something like: "Please send your chat messages publically to the group. However, if you need to communicate privately to someone on the facilitation team, select the *all panelists* option from the drop down menu."

Factors That Influence Chat

How the chat feature is used in your session will depend on several factors, including how audio is transmitted, whether or not you are working with a cofacilitator or producer, and group size. Each of these factors is examined in detail below:

How Audio Selection Influences Chat   The features in a virtual classroom are interrelated, so any decision regarding how audio is transmitted influences how the chat area is used and how much. When audio is delivered as one-way voice over internet protocol (VoIP), only the facilitator(s) communicates verbally and the participants listen and respond using the chat feature exclusively. Conversely, if a session is conducted with two-way audio (either through a phone line or VoIP), the frequency of chat is lower since participants have alternate

---

CHAT TIPS

1. Work with a producer to manage the chat area.
2. Tell participants at the beginning of the session that the facilitation team is monitoring the chat area and to please use it.
3. When responding to a participant, use his/her first name so it's clear which message you are responding to.
4. Chat deliberately and repeat key phrases of the question so it's obvious which message you are responding to.
5. Create a text file with links, questions, key messages so you can cut and paste directly into the chat box.
6. Let participants answer each other's questions when possible.
7. If the chat area is very active, don't try to respond to every comment or question. Look for themes, and address comments collectively.

ways to communicate. See Table 2-2, "Audio Options for Virtual Classrooms," for a review of common ways to transmit audio in a virtual classroom.

How the Number of Facilitators Influences Chat   An additional facilitator (or producer) opens up many possibilities for managing a virtual session. Here are a few typical options.

- While one facilitator presents the content, the other facilitator manages the chat area.
- The lead facilitator presents the content and a producer/cofacilitator manages the chat box (see Table 4-3, "Facilitator and Producer Tasks During a Virtual Classroom Session," for more on this combination). If there are questions that the producer/cofacilitator cannot answer, they are passed to the lead facilitator.
- Facilitators sharing the content presentation duties also share the producer/facilitator duties.

In the case of a facilitator working alone, the best option is to pause periodically to review the comments posted in the chat area and, if possible, respond verbally. Facilitators can respond to other chat messages and questions while participants are working on an exercise or taking a break.

TIP

Roger Courville, author of *The Virtual Presenter's Handbook*

Some facilitators describe a sense of loss when they first facilitate in the virtual classroom because they cannot see participants. But if you think about it, the virtual classroom offers one-to-one intimacy that you don't have in the traditional classroom. For example, in a virtual classroom with 50 participants, if you ask for a show of hands, you get an exact number, not an estimate like you would in a traditional classroom of the same size. In a virtual classroom, you can ask a large audience to type a response to a chat question and get simultaneous responses. If you did this in the traditional classroom, it would be mayhem.

How the Size of Your Audience Influences Chat   A small audience with two-way audio and a highly interactive discussion via audio will result in a limited use of the chat area, while a large audience with one-way audio results in a much greater use of the chat area. Maximizing the use of the chat area with a large audience or an audience with one-way audio is a great way to keep participants engaged.

Using Polls

Chapter 5, "Developing Virtual Classroom Training," covered how to design well-written polls. This chapter describes how to time and comment on poll results and broadcast them to participants. Note that you should take advantage of any capability offered in your virtual classroom to build your polls prior to your session. Taking this proactive route will greatly smooth the integration of polling into your session.

Timing and Commenting on Poll Results

If you are working with a producer, decide up front who will be in charge of posting the polls and when the polls should be posted. Ensure that it's noted in the facilitator guide. Inserting a slide with the title or subject of the poll at the appropriate place in your presentation and including notes about the timing and commenting responsibility in your facilitator guide, will ensure that polling goes smoothly. It's also important to ensure that you have something to say about the poll results. It seems an obvious point, but *pointless polling* is an all too common practice, and it may have a negative impact on learner engagement. To prevent pointless polling, the facilitator should be prepared with an appropriate response and segue to the next activity and be prepared to comment on unexpected results.

Broadcasting Poll Results

Generally, the results of a poll are broadcast instantly as the participants respond or at a specific time chosen by the facilitator. How you use the broadcast feature depends on your learning objectives. If you are polling about demographics, for example, the number of years of experience a participant has worked at the organization, it makes sense to display results instantly. Knowledge checks and opinion polls are more effective if the results are delayed to get more "honest' answers from participants. Delaying the broadcast also gives the learner more time to reflect on the question. No matter which technique you choose, include instructions in the facilitator guide to indicate how and when you will broadcast results.

RECORD YOURSELF AND IMPROVE

Virtual classroom facilitators looking for ways to improve their "game" should follow the lead of top athletes and study "replays" of their performances to identify opportunities for improvement. Recording your session in the virtual classroom is generally a simple process and, once you have captured a performance, review it with these questions in mind.

- **Voice intonation and pacing:** Did you vary the tone, pitch, and speed of your voice sufficiently to keep the participants interested?
- **Clarity of speech:** Were your instructions clearly understood by the participants when you gave instructions for an exercise?
- **Interactivity:** Did you use the interactive features in your classroom every few minutes?
- **Chat comments:** Did you incorporate participant comments and questions posted in the chat area into your session? Did you encourage participants to chat?
- **Screen annotation:** Did you annotate the screen while you were speaking to emphasize key points?

Use Table 3-2, "Virtual Classroom Observation Template," to capture your self-evaluation notes.

Some facilitators may find it difficult to listen to their recorded voice, but it's a very useful tool for improvement. I recently listened to a recording of my virtual classroom session and found that I needed to slow the pace of my speech. I also discovered a typo on a slide and identified a segment of the session that needed more interactivity. If you work with sensitive content or for some reason cannot record a live classroom session, record yourself without participants. You'll still find the exercise extremely useful even without the live audience.

CONCLUSION

Facilitating in the virtual classroom requires a combination of techniques from traditional classroom training plus new methods unique to the virtual classroom environment. Keep in mind the following techniques.

Checklist of Facilitation Techniques

✓ Set a positive tone for early engagement with participants.
✓ Work with a producer to maximize interactions with participants.
✓ Use vocal variety and speak with expression.
✓ Don't forget to pause.
✓ Keep your energy level high.
✓ Use clear language.
✓ Annotate the screen to support your spoken word.
✓ Use virtual classroom features to obtain participant feedback.
✓ Scan the entire screen to look for participant feedback.
✓ Practice using virtual classroom features so you can use them seamlessly.
✓ Listen to recordings of your virtual classroom sessions to improve your performance.

CONTINUOUS LEARNING

1. Listen to radio talk show hosts and note the pace, clarity, and intonation of pitch in their voices.
2. Ask your producer for feedback after your next session. Define ahead of time of the areas on which you would like her to focus.

3. Attend virtual classroom training as a participant and keep a journal of facilitation ideas and notes. Refer to them next time you need to refresh your facilitation techniques.

4. If you have children, the next time you read a children's story read it with passion, varying your pace and tone to practice these techniques.

5. Visit this book's website to watch videoclips of the facilitation techniques described in this chapter.

References

Borg, James. *Body Language: 7 Easy Lessons to Master the Silent Language*. Upper Saddle River, NJ: Pearson Education, 2008.

Christopher, Darlene. "Facilitating in the Virtual Classroom: How to Compensate for the Lack of Body Language." In *The 2012 Pfeiffer Annual: Training*, ed. Elaine Biech, 131–139. San Francisco: John Wiley & Sons, 2012.

Medina, John. *Brain Rules*. Seattle: Pear Press, 2008.

Miner, Nanette. "The Non-Drowsy Virtual Classroom." *T&D Magazine*. July 2009, 31–33.

Turmel, Wayne. *10 Steps to Successful Virtual Presentations*. Alexandria, VA: ASTD Press, 2011.

SEVEN

Putting It All Together with the PREP Model

HERE'S HOW TO:

- Apply the PREP Model to your virtual classroom session.
- Plan successful virtual classroom training.
- Rehearse effectively to prepare for a live session.
- Execute a live session.
- Conduct a postsession review.

THE PREP MODEL

The PREP Model: Plan, Rehearse, Execute, and Postsession Review, is a framework for designing and delivering successful virtual classroom training programs. It allows instructional designers, facilitators, producers, and course administrators to accomplish world class virtual training sessions by aligning their virtual training design and development process with the four distinct project phases discussed in this chapter (see Figure 7-1).

Plan

Nothing is more important than the planning phase. Note also that strict compliance to the order of the tasks outlined in the planning phase is not as

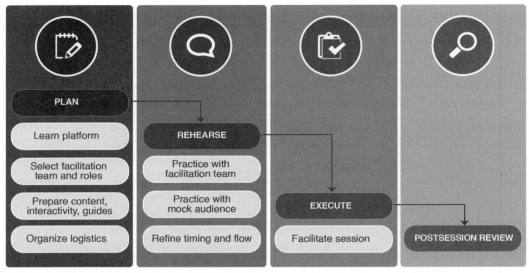

Figure 7-1 Diagram of the PREP Model.

important as ensuring that each task is accomplished. If you've read this book in chapter order, you'll recognize the first three tasks were covered in Chapter 3, "Getting Started," Chapter 4, "The Virtual Classroom Team and the Members' Roles," and Chapter 5, "Developing Virtual Classroom Training." These chapters include tips on becoming comfortable using a virtual classroom platform, a discussion of team members and their roles, an exploration of content design, and the importance of interactivity, along with general guidelines for both facilitators and participants. This chapter reviews these tasks and includes information on organizing logistics. Let's look more closely at the individual steps in the planning phase.

Learn Platform

The first task is getting comfortable with the virtual classroom platform you're using so that your focus remains on the subject matter you are delivering, not the technology. This is a vitally important point! A facilitator who demonstrates inexperience with the toolsets she is using dampens the enthusiasm and confidence learners have for the facilitator and the viability of virtual training. Review Chapter 3, "Getting Started," to see a variety of options for learning how to use and get comfortable with unfamiliar virtual training technology.

Select Facilitation Team and Roles

Typically, a facilitation team consists of a facilitator and a producer who work together to deliver the training and engage the audience. The facilitator advances the slides and engages the audience verbally, while the producer monitors the chat feature and sets up exercises and polls. If the event is particularly complex, you can add additional facilitators and producers to handle the work. See Chapter 4, "The Virtual Classroom Team and the Members' Roles," for complete details on the roles and needed skills of both the facilitator and producer.

Prepare Content, Interactivity, and Guides

Instructors often adapt existing classroom content for the virtual classroom. In fact, much of the training delivered via virtual classroom stems directly from content originally delivered via face-to-face training. If you get this assignment, the first step is to select the essential content for the live virtual session. Do this by identifying the content appropriate for pre- and postsession work, so that the live time is reserved for more exercises and interactivity with participants.

Keeping participants engaged is vital, so well-planned exercises that offer sufficient interactivity are essential. Convert your traditional classroom multiple-choice, true-or-false, and oral questions to poll questions. Small group work is easily converted to breakout room sessions if your virtual classroom tool has this feature. Use the chat area to solicit responses to open-ended questions. Participants "raise" their hands in a virtual classroom by changing their "status" and virtual whiteboard activity looks and feels like the work done in traditional classrooms. See Chapter 5, "Developing Virtual Classroom Training" for more details and Chapter 9, "Ideas for Icebreakers and Exercises," for some specific ideas for the virtual classroom.

After modifying the content and exercises, develop the support materials, including workbooks, job aids, and handouts. Just like support materials designed for in-person training, your virtual classroom support materials should be checked for clarity, consistency, and accuracy.

The facilitator guide is a written set of instructions that describe how the content will be covered. Each slide is accompanied by a description (or image) of what the participants' see when the facilitator is speaking. It also describes how the features of the virtual classroom are used to execute exercises and interactivity. Build a timeline into the script to ensure that the material is covered in the allotted time.

Organize Logistics

In addition to time and date, a logistical plan should detail how the participants will access course materials, the location of the facilitator and session audience, and technical details, such as how the audio will be transmitted. If you are working with global participants, other logistical considerations apply. See Chapter 8, "Working with Global Participants," for further discussion of these points.

Time and Date   Select the time and date for your session(s) based on the participants' perspectives. If they are in different time zones, select a time and date that matches their business hours and work schedules. Pay attention to the date(s) of your course to make sure you are not conflicting with a national or religious holiday or another day that impacts participants (e.g., department retreat or quarterly earnings meeting).

Materials   Determining how participants will access course materials is another important step. Options include posting materials on a course website, uploading materials to the virtual training platform for participants to download, emailing materials as attachments to participants, or physically mailing the materials. Whichever option you choose, provide clear instructions

> **TIP**
> If you have large files to send to participants, post them online using tools like Google Drive or DropBox and tell participants how to download them to their computers.

on what the participants need to do before class (e.g., which materials should be printed and brought to the session).

Delivery Room and Equipment   The next step is to determine the location from which to deliver your session. Some organizations have a room dedicated to distance learning programs. If your organization has such a facility, someone in the organization is probably assigned to the room (such as an IT specialist) to provide support. Set up a meeting with the training facility IT person (or other dedicated staff) to discuss the session and ways to ensure that the technology aspect of the session goes smoothly.

If you don't have a dedicated room for delivering virtual training, plan to deliver your session from a location that has at least one wired Internet connection for the facilitator or producer's computer. Relying completely on a wireless Internet connection is a risky option, since near 100 percent reliability is harder to predict. The room should be equipped with a computer or laptop for each member of the facilitation team and a separate computer showing the view of a logged-in participant.

If you're using VoIP audio, then facilitators need a quality USB connect headset with noise cancelation to ensure high quality audio transmission. If you plan to use a traditional phone conference call setup for audio, then you'll need a telephone with a headset. Consider using a speaker phone with multiple extension microphones if more than one person will be participating in the call from the room.

TIP

Todd Slater, Technology Learning Center Program Director, The Nature Conservancy

If you use a conference call for audio, request that the beeps that indicate a person has joined or left the call be turned off. Otherwise, it's very distracting to hear the beeps when people join or drop off the call. It also makes it easier to talk to participants who want to stay on the line a few minutes after the session ends to discuss a topic.

PARTICIPANT PREPARATION CHECKLIST

Participants often remain in their workspace when they attend virtual classroom training. Coworkers and even supervisors may not think twice about interrupting them because it may simply appear that they are listening to music on their headphones while doing work on their computer.

   To maximize audience engagement and promote learning transfer, share the tips below with your audience before the session so they know what to expect and are prepared to make the most of their time in the virtual classroom. For example:

✓ Test your computer a few days before the actual session. Follow the instructions sent to you by the facilitation team to make sure you can access the virtual classroom.

✓ Log in to the virtual classroom session 10 minutes early, so that you are ready to go when the class begins.

✓ Post a "do-not-disturb" sign or an "in-training" sign on your office door or the back of your chair. Respect your learning time and get your coworkers to respect your time as well, so you can focus on professional development.

✓ Turn your mobile phone to vibrate. This will help to prevent interruptions during the live session.

✓ Eliminate email and instant message interruptions. Disable chimes and pop ups that indicate the arrival of an email message or close email completely. Create an "out-of-office" message so that people who email you during the class won't expect an immediate response. Set your instant message tool to "do not disturb" or turn it off completely.

✓ Use the "Stepped Away" feature (if available) if you need to temporarily leave the session so that the facilitator doesn't call on you while you are gone.

Finally, make sure you have enough electrical outlets (and extension cords) to keep laptop computers charged, with a mouse for each one.

Participants' Audio   Most virtual classroom tools offer a choice of VoIP, built in teleconferencing, or both. If the participants will be in an open office

---

TIP

Develop a communication strategy regarding virtual classroom session reminders. For example, send three reminders: One the day the person enrolls; one the day before the session; and one a few hours before the session start time. Each reminder should include instructions on how to test computers for readiness, the session date/start time, and a participant preparation checklist.

---

area and you plan to use VoIP, make sure each participant has a computer headset to listen to the audio so they will not disturb coworkers. Test the VoIP prior to the session. This is especially important in low-bandwidth locations.

Participant Computer Check   Send instructions to participants prior to the session to give them enough time to install plug-ins and deal with firewall or other access issues. Most virtual tool vendors offer a website with an automatic participant computer check to ensure that each user's computer has the right plug-in, audio capability, and so on. Use this utility if available.

If participants are new to the virtual classroom and you think they may have trouble accessing the virtual classroom, plan a brief orientation session.

TIP

Michelle Hall, eLearning & Multimedia Team Lead at the U.S. Department of Energy National Training Center

When someone signs up for one of our virtual classroom trainings, our learning analyst contacts each enrollee via email and asks for their IT point of contact. Then the enrollee is required to complete a 45-minute course: Introduction to Distance Learning. The purpose of the course is twofold: (1) We test their connection with WebEx so we can troubleshoot any technical issues in advance. Since we have the name of their IT person, we can contact that person if needed. (2) We also show enrollees how to interact using whiteboard, chat, and polls so they are comfortable with the technology.

Invite learners to a virtual classroom session to ensure that they can access the meeting room, see the visuals on the screen and hear the audio. You can also cover a brief introduction of the virtual classroom interactivity features.

The more thorough and exhaustive your planning is, the more successful your virtual classroom session will be. The tasks and relevant questions to ask for each aspect of the virtual classroom are summarized in Table 7-1. Note that the entire PREP Model Checklist can be found in Appendix H.

Rehearsing

Even if you've mastered the course material through numerous face-to-face deliveries, rehearsal is important when you move to the virtual classroom. Remember, you'll have to adjust your language pace and use the interactive features in place of familiar body language cues. Rehearsing also gives the facilitator and producer an opportunity to work together to coordinate the moving parts of a virtual classroom to ensure the session flows smoothly. The rehearsal is one of the easiest ways to determine where to adjust and correct content and exercises. If you don't have time to rehearse, then set expectations appropriately by calling your first session a "pilot" session.

TIP

Use the recording feature in your virtual classroom if you cannot rehearse with others. Listen to yourself and note areas that need adjusting.

Where to Rehearse

Rehearse in the environment where the actual training will be delivered and use the same equipment that you will use for your live session. If the training will be delivered from a conference room, then rehearse from the conference room. If the training will be delivered from home, then rehearse from home. It's essential that the rehearsal conditions mimic real world conditions as closely as possible.

Table 7-1 Planning Checklist

Learn Platform
✓ Identify the virtual classroom tool (software application) that best suits your training needs.
✓ Learn the features and functionality of the tool and how they work.
✓ Understand the limitations of the tool (maximum number of participants, hosts, etc.).
✓ Understand audio options available (VoIP, integrated conference call).

Select Facilitation Team and Roles
✓ Identify a facilitator who knows how to engage virtual participants.
✓ Identify an instructional designer who has experience with virtual classroom design.
✓ Identify a producer to partner with the facilitator.
✓ Determine division of labor and roles between the facilitator and producer.
✓ Select a course administrator to handle event planning.
✓ Identify IT support.

Prepare Content, Interactivity Exercises and Guides
✓ Divide content into prework and postwork, leaving discussion and topics that require a facilitator's input for the time spent in the virtual classroom session.
✓ Incorporate features of the virtual classroom into the design appropriately, with interactivity every 3 to 5 minutes (e.g., polls, whiteboarding chat, exercises).
✓ Offer a variety of exercises that appeal to different learning styles and personalities.
✓ Develop slides that cover one key concept each and include appropriate images, videos, and other instructional materials.
✓ Develop a facilitator guide that describes what material will be covered as each slide or other content appears, actions the facilitator and producer will take, and a detailed timeline.
✓ Develop participant workbooks and other supporting materials that are clear, consistent and accurate.

Organize Logistics
✓ Select session start and end times that match the working hours and work days of participants.
✓ Send course materials to participants with instructions on how to access them.
✓ Identify optimal audio option for training (VoIP, integrated conference call).
✓ Select audio transmission type (teleconference, VoIP) and test with the facilitation team and participants.
✓ Secure a location and equipment for the facilitation team to use to deliver the session.

Likewise, rehearse with the computer or laptop that will be used for the live session. Some virtual classroom tools require a plug-in download. If that's the case, downloading (or worse, failing to download) during your session is very disrupting. Test the microphone or telephone conference service that you plan to use. Ask a coworker to connect to the virtual classroom and listen for a few minutes to check the sound and make adjustments so that the system delivers clear audio.

How to Rehearse

Step 1: Practice with the Facilitation Team   Start by practicing with the facilitation team and getting used to member roles and responsibilities. Agree on the sequence of each topic, identify who will be responsible for each activity, and decide what each person will do and say. Your facilitator guide should contain this information and should be followed as you rehearse. Note any missing and unclear information in the guide and make necessary revisions.

During rehearsal, make sure that the facilitator and producer become familiar with the slides. This is especially important if someone other than the facilitator, such as an instructional designer, created the slides. Both the facilitator and producer should know which slides have slide builds (such as bullet points entering the slide one by one) to ensure smooth delivery during the session. It detracts from the training if when faced with an unfamiliar slide, the facilitator says: "Oh never mind that slide, I'm not sure what that slide is for anyway" or "Oh, I already covered that."

Step 2: Rehearse with a Mock Audience   Once the facilitation team is comfortable with the session content, practice with a mock audience of subject matter experts, coworkers, or people interested in the topic who cannot attend the live session.

Engage fully with the mock audience and use the session to practice working with the interactive features of the virtual classroom. To solicit useful feedback that will help you to improve your session, provide your mock audience with the "Rehearsal Feedback Form" in Appendix G. Instruct participants to approach the session as if they are true course participants and to provide feedback accordingly.

TIP

Karen Hyder, co-author of *The eLearning Guild's Handbook on Synchronous eLearning*

Don't rest on your laurels. Delivering successful virtual classroom sessions requires more than just skills and experience. The preparation is equally as important. You have to log in, rehearse, and prepare every single time.

If you are pressed for time and cannot rehearse a full session, practice the first three minutes and the exercises. Rehearse the first three minutes so that they are flawless and energetic to set a positive tone for the session. In addition, focus on the exercises and interactive parts of the session. This will help assure you that instructions are clear, that you are comfortable with the interactive features of the classroom, and that sufficient time is allocated for each part.

Step 3: Incorporating Feedback   After rehearsing, gather the facilitation team to review the rehearsal feedback forms, notes from the facilitation team, and comments in the chat area. Whenever possible, schedule time to incorporate feedback from the rehearsal into your materials immediately after the mock rehearsal. Otherwise, you may not remember what your notes meant and you may lose valuable information gathered.

Start at the beginning of the session and open electronic versions of your materials (e.g., slides and participant and facilitator guides). Note exactly where changes need to be incorporated into the materials. You might need to follow up with a particular mock audience member to clarify a comment, so make sure mock participants put their name and contact information on the feedback form. Use the rehearsal checklist in Table 7-2 as a guide to ensure you are ready for the next phase: Execute.

Execute

It's finally here—the moment you have been planning for—the live virtual classroom session. If you have planned and rehearsed, you are on your way to a successful virtual classroom session.

Table 7-2 Rehearsal Checklist

> ✓   Rehearse with facilitation team (e.g., facilitator and producer), so everyone is clear on who does what, who says what, and the timing of content/exercises.
> ✓   Rehearse with a mock audience to verify that the content is clear and the exercises make sense.
> ✓   Test audio transmission (teleconference, VoIP) with the facilitation team and mock audience.
> ✓   Rehearse in the location that will be used for the formal launch.
> ✓   Practice the first three minutes until they are flawless and energetic to set a positive tone for the session.
> ✓   Fix the problem areas identified during rehearsal (e.g., update slides or correct the facilitator guide).

Facilitators who are familiar with in-person training know the importance of arriving early to check the room setup, materials, and other details. The same technique applies to the virtual classroom. The facilitation team should log on at least 30 minutes before the session start time to do an audio check and engage in last minute strategizing or preparation.

While counting down to the start of your session and the arrival of the participants, check that all your materials are loaded into the virtual classroom and working properly. As the participants begin to arrive use this housekeeping checklist before starting:

✓   Welcome each participant as they enter the room.
✓   Test audio to make sure each participant can hear you and you can hear them. Get them used to speaking.
✓   Practice muting and unmuting audio with participants.
✓   Describe how to download the handouts.
✓   Use the chat feature with participants to socialize and get to know them.
✓   Call, send an instant message or email to enrollees who have not arrived.

TIP

When you send an electronic calendar invitation to the facilitation team members, add 30 minutes prior to the session start time to take care of last-minute issues and 30 minutes after the actual end time to conduct a postsession review.

Additionally, consider engaging with participants beyond simply technical checks. A few simple activities to do as you countdown to the start of your session include:

1. Conduct a poll to gain background information about the participants.
2. Share related information about your event (related courses, related resources) on a slide with links.
3. Post a presession slide show as described in Chapter 5, "Developing Virtual Classroom Training." Design the slides with statistics, quotes, or other interesting information that relates to your content on slides.
4. Play a word game.

Of course, the rest of your session should continue with a high level of engagement. Refer to Chapter 6, "Facilitation Techniques," for a range of techniques that the facilitator and producer can utilize to maintain a high level of interaction throughout a session.

Have a Plan "B" and Keep Your Cool

Picture this: A new online facilitator has spent weeks designing and rehearsing for his first virtual classroom session and is eager to make a good first impression. The facilitator wants to demonstrate that a virtual classroom solution is valid and can be successfully rolled out to multiple global locations. As the session starts, the facilitator loses Internet connectivity and access to the virtual meeting room. Since the facilitator has a conference call, an audio connection to the participants is still available. In a panic, the facilitator blurts out "I guess this isn't going to work after all. Why do these things always happen to ME?"

A skilled online facilitator knows that from time to time technology glitches will happen and has a plan to deal coolly and confidently with these issues. If you partner with a producer, as described in Chapter 4, "The Virtual Classroom Team and the Members' Roles," you will be ready for these technical challenges. Always make sure you can access the meeting agenda and handouts outside of the meeting room (either with printed copies or a copy on your computer), so that you can continue the meeting on a phone line if necessary.

> # TIP
> **Cindy Huggett, author of *The Virtual Training Guidebook***
>
> Even if you think you don't need a producer because you are a very experienced virtual classroom facilitator, it's still a good idea to have one. If you have just one technical glitch with a participant that takes you a few minutes to resolve, you can lose momentum. Your class will go so much more smoothly with a producer helping you.
>
> One time while facilitating a class from my home office, my power went out for about 30 seconds, and I lost connectivity to the session. We were right in the middle of an activity and the producer was able to seamlessly keep it going while I logged back in. If I had been the only one there, the activity would have stopped, participants would have lost focus, and the class would have been disrupted. Having a producer made the difference.

Emailing training materials to participants prior to the session also ensures that you all have common materials to refer to as a backup.

In the previous scenario, a good strategy would have been for the facilitator to tell the audience to standby for a moment, mute the audio, and find a solution with the producer. The producer could have investigated the cause of the technical problem while the facilitator began introducing the agenda, housekeeping items, and the first topic.

If the facilitator had planned how to shift from plan "A" to plan "B" with the producer before the session, the shift would have been flawless. The participants would have certainly noticed that things weren't going exactly as planned, but they would have also observed a professional who was well prepared and confident in a difficult situation.

"Mise en Place" for the Virtual Classroom Facilitation Team

Foodies and chefs will recognize the French phrase, "mise en place" (pronounced MEEZ ahn plahs), which translates to "everything in its place." In the world of cooking, it means having all your ingredients prepared and ready to go *before* you start cooking. It's tempting to jump right in and turn on the stove as soon as your first few ingredients are ready to go. But great chefs know that it pays to prepare everything in advance to prevent problems and avoid chaos in the kitchen when it's time to put meals together.

If you facilitate in the virtual classroom, there are factors that can derail a session. Some are out of the facilitator's control, but others can be mitigated. One key to successful training in the virtual classroom is meticulous planning and preparation before the session, just like the mise en place technique.

Consider everything you need to prepare before you say "welcome" to your virtual audience and start your session, including the following.

1. **Print your digital materials**. Make sure you have a printed copy of all the materials you will be using in your session. For example, have your facilitator guide handy, as well as a copy of the participant workbook.
2. **Print a list of participants.** The list should contain name, photo (if available), job title, location, and whatever other information will help you remember who is who.
3. **Open up websites or online tools that you plan to show during the session**. Do this before the session starts to make sure web links are on hand and everything is working properly.
4. **Turn off applications you won't use.** Turn off applications such as email. This will help to improve the response time of the virtual classroom tool. Turning off instant messaging tools also prevents messages from appearing on the screen for all to see if you use the screen sharing feature. If you need to leave your email application or instant message tool open, make sure to disable email pop ups and audio alerts indicating that a new message has arrived.
5. **Conduct an audio check.** Before participants begin arriving into the virtual classroom, make sure that your audio is working properly. Ask a coworker to join your session as a participant to help you conduct a brief test.
6. **Turn mobiles phone to vibrate.** All mobile devices in the session delivery room should be on vibrate or off to prevent interruptions during the live session.

7. **Review plan B.** Think of everything that could go wrong, and plan a response. Have a backup computer, backup headset or phone, screen shots of any applications or websites you plan to show. My building has biannual fire drills, so I'll even go so far as to check with security to see if a fire drill is planned so I can prepare for that potential disruption.

8. **Create a list of contact names for technical support.** When you need technical assistance, speed is essential. If you have contact names ready at your fingertips, you will be one step closer to resolving the problem.

9. **Eliminate distractions.** Close your door and put a sign on it that indicates you are running a training session.

10. **Prepare postsession materials.** If you plan to send an online evaluation, prepare it in advance. Or, if you plan to send follow-up materials, prepare an email in draft form so you can send it right away, while the course material is fresh in everyone's mind.

To Record or Not to Record

Recording virtual classroom training is usually just a matter of learning how to use the recording feature to record a session, then retrieving the recording. Recording a session enables the facilitator to provide a distributed and "training-on-demand" solution to reach more learners.

Recording a session can be beneficial. The **_real_** question to ask, however, is whether or not it makes sense to record and how the recording could impact the live session. Think about it this way: What if you brought a video camera to a face-to-face training session and announced to participants that you will be recording the training, then sharing the recording with nonattendees. Would participants behave differently because of the camera in the room?

While recording training in a virtual classroom is much more subtle, thinking through the impact and privacy considerations of recording a session is worthwhile. Here are few items to consider.

1. **Tell participants they are being recorded.** Announce at the beginning of the session that you are recording and explain how the recording will be used and who will have access to it.

2. **Encourage people to attend the live session.** Don't offer the recording to people as a substitute for participating in the live virtual classroom. Offer the recording to those who may need to leave early or to those who participated and want to review some sections of the course.

3. **Record sessions that focus on process, policies, and systems.** Sessions that are business oriented are good candidates for recording. Examples include training on software or web applications or training on a new industry regulation or sales policy.

4. **Use discretion when recording sessions that encourage self-reflection, personal stories.** Participants who share personal stories or experiences can often provide insight of great value to colleagues, whether in leadership training, career management, communications, or conflict resolution training. To encourage participants to contribute such personal experiences, facilitators may institute the "Vegas Rule"—noting "what is shared in the classroom stays in the classroom" to ensure confidentiality. Likewise, these types of sessions are not appropriate for recording.

5. **Edit the recording.** Most virtual classroom platforms include an editing feature that allows you to cut sections of the recording that you don't need. For example, the final version of the recording should start at the moment the facilitator starts with the content of the session. Remove the first few minutes of the recording when participants are still logging in. Also remove sections of the recording when participants are working individually on an exercise and there is silence or when participants are taking a break.

Postsession Review

Celebrate! You did it! After you celebrate your successful virtual classroom session, take a moment to work on these tasks.

Gather Feedback from Participants

Gathering feedback from participants is easy to do. It is usually done using an online evaluation conducted at the conclusion of the training. Develop an evaluation plan in advance. Some virtual classroom tools offer built-in online

---

VIRTUAL CLASSROOM EVALUATION

In addition to the areas you traditionally evaluate for in-person training, consider asking participants to evaluate:

1. Pace of the session
2. Amount of interactivity
3. Usefulness of the exercises
4. Skill of the facilitator
5. Skill of the producer
6. Effectiveness of the virtual format

---

survey functionality you can use to develop your feedback form. Or, if your
organization uses an online survey tool like SurveyMonkey, direct participants
to the survey link before the course ends. Lower the barrier to getting this feedback by setting aside time for it during your session and making it as easy as
possible—just a single mouse click on a survey link.

Also, prepare an email message with the online evaluation information
ready to send to participants at the conclusion of the session. Even if you ask
participants to complete the survey at the conclusion of the session, some
may be pressed for time and won't take the time to complete it, so the email
message is your back up.

Gather Feedback from the Virtual Classroom Team

The other component of the postsession review step is debriefing the facilitation team immediately after the training concludes. Experience is the best
teacher, so take time to reflect with your team after your session ends about
what worked well and what could be improved Make the changes to your facilitator script and slides right away, while the ideas are fresh.

The best way to make sure this important step of debriefing the session is
accomplished is to schedule it ahead of time. Add thirty minutes to the end of
the scheduled classroom time and invite anyone who played a role to partici-

---

TIP

Debra Moore, Instructional Systems Designer, Defense Acquisition University

An easy way to gain valuable feedback on the design of your virtual classroom session is to invite another designer to join the session as a participant and then share ideas on how to increase engagement, improve slide design, or adjust an exercise.

---

pate (see Chapter 4, "The Virtual Classroom Team and the Members' Roles"). Review all aspects of the training, including registration, content and materials, facilitation, timing, interactive exercises, and class size.

You may already have some feedback to share with the team if participants responded to your online evaluation at the end of the session. Review the survey results online during your debriefing session and include them as part of the discussion. If you don't get results immediately, make sure to send them to the virtual classroom team once they have been compiled.

Save Your Chat Text

The chat text from your virtual classroom session is a goldmine of information. If the chat area was well utilized throughout the session, it becomes an

---

When your session ends, remember to:

1. Download and/or capture attendance.
2. Convert chat to FAQs.
3. Collect evaluation results.
4. Debrief with facilitation team.
5. Download poll results.
6. Post recording.
7. Email follow-up materials to participants.

EXPECT THE UNEXPECTED IN THE VIRTUAL CLASSROOM

While interviewing people for this book, I came across many unexpected and funny incidents that happened to virtual classroom facilitators and producers. For a dose of this humor and wisdom, read on.

1. Someone called into the virtual classroom conference call and asked if anyone had ordered a pizza.
2. A producer thought she was on mute after finishing an especially difficult session. Her son walked into her home office and she told him she needed a hug. The participants who were still online started sending her chat messages with virtual "hugs."
3. A participant was overheard ordering a refrigerator and microwave from an appliance store in the background when he thought he was on mute.
4. A facilitation team was delivering a session from a conference room when sirens began sounding because a fire drill for the building was in progress.
5. A presenter forgot to close Skype and then moved into application sharing mode. While she was doing a demonstration of an online tool her boyfriend sent a romantic message via Skype that popped up on the screen for all to see.
6. A presenter was talking from his mobile phone and dropped his car off at a repair shop during a session. He forgot to mute his phone, so the entire class heard the discussion.
7. A facilitator was delivering her session from her home office and using a webcam when her cat jumped up on the back of her chair, surprising her and the participants.
8. A participant started changing into gym clothes in front of his computer after a session, but he forgot to turn off his webcam.
9. The facilitation team discovered that one of the participants was attending a virtual classroom session while simultaneously working as a bank teller in a drive-through window. The participant forgot to mute her phone and started helping a customer.
10. A presenter had been working on her resume before starting a session. When she moved into application sharing mode and shared her desktop, her resume appeared on the screen for all to see, including her boss who was observing the session.

important artifact of the session. Here are a few ways to use the chat text after your session concludes.

1. Review the chat text to see how well the facilitator and/or producer responded to and summarized comments and questions.
2. Share the chat text with other facilitators who will lead similar sessions so they can get a feel for the types of comments and questions to expect.
3. Turn the questions and answers provided into FAQs and post online.

Ask the producer to type the participant questions into the chat area before participants start responding to make this chat review easier to do. Depending on how and where you post the FAQs online, you can create a more permanent home for the content and make it visible to those not able to attend your session.

CONTINUOUS LEARNING

1. Conduct a walkthrough of your session and identify areas where you need to develop a backup plan.
2. Sign up for a virtual classroom training or webinar and review the instructions you receive to help you prepare for the session. Note what information is most helpful and what is missing and adjust your instructions for learners accordingly.
3. Interview virtual classroom facilitators and producers and ask them how they prepare for a live session and how they rehearse for the session.
4. Review the planning and rehearsal checklists. What else can you add that will ensure your session runs smoothly?
5. Read the chat text after your session ends. What can you learn from participants' questions to improve your next session?

Fine-Tuning

EIGHT

Working with Global Participants

HERE'S HOW TO:

- Collect key information about international target audiences.
- Adjust facilitation techniques to match the needs of global audiences.
- Adapt your use of virtual classroom features to maximize learning transfer for participants from different cultures.

Despite the continuing globalization of business, only 29 percent of companies surveyed in a 2008 ASTD report entitled *Learning's Role in Globally Dispersed Workforces* characterized their global learning initiatives as successful. According to the report, two of the key barriers to implementing effective global learning initiatives were budgetary constraints and a lack of qualified training staff.

This statistic may be one of the reasons companies are increasingly turning to virtual classroom training as a way to cut costs while simultaneously increasing the frequency of training. Here's a scenario that illustrates why a company would choose this training strategy.

SCENARIO: GLOBAL OPERATIONS NEED A GLOBAL VIRTUAL CLASSROOM

A North American firm with offices in six locations in one country purchases a European firm with offices in four other countries. As a result of the acquisition, the parent company needs to merge several human resources management systems, including the performance management system and learning management system. In addition, the company must train the European human resources departments on how the systems work. Previously, when the company offered similar training, employees traveled to company headquarters. The acquisition created a truly global company, so bringing employees to headquarters is prohibitively expensive. As a result, the company asks its training department to design and deliver training in a global virtual classroom.

The challenge for the training department in this scenario is twofold: (1) Figure out how to transition from a traditional classroom to a virtual one and (2) Transition from training groups of national participants sharing a similar national heritage and perspective to training groups of international participants with different cultural perspectives. The previous chapters of this book addressed the first challenge; this chapter addresses the second.

CONSIDER THE NEEDS OF GLOBAL PARTICIPANTS

Imagine you are an American who's been asked to join a virtual classroom. The instructor begins the presentation by displaying an image of a cricket game in progress on your screen and says: "*Sometimes dealing with the pressures at work feels like a game of 20/20 limited cricket when you're chasing a score of 220 and it's the last over. Then, to make it worse you are facing the best fast bowler and you only have one wicket in hand!*" Since there are only 25,000 active cricket players in the United States according to the sport's official association website (USACA.org), a cricket analogy is the wrong choice because most participants would not understand it.

Or consider this scenario. Imagine you are living in a part of the world where the work week is not based on the standard Western-style Monday through Friday (for example, some parts of the Middle East) and the virtual training class you need to take is only offered on Friday, which is a weekend for you. Would this lack of sensitivity to the cultural norms of your country make you feel like a valued employee of the company?

While you might think these or similar scenarios are rare, you'd be surprised how many times virtual training content includes inappropriate cultural or country-specific references that don't consider cultural traditions, such as different workdays or business hours.

To truly meet the needs of global participants, virtual classroom designers and facilitators need to think about *every* aspect of the training from the learners' perspectives and make appropriate adjustments to their course design and execution.

COLLECT AUDIENCE INFORMATION

To avoid situations such as the previous scenario, gather as much information as possible from remote participants before initiating your training. Potential sources for this information might include local site managers and human resources personnel, members of the local site learning team and IT staff, and even members of the target audience. Here are five core areas of inquiry to consider.

Language

Determine the range of languages spoken by the participants and whether the group shares fluency (and what level of fluency) in a common language, such as English. In addition, ask if the participants have experience attending virtual training delivered in English. This information will help you determine how to adjust and clarify your spoken language and text on the materials provided.

Cultural Differences

In a global training environment, participants bring an added dimension of expectations tied to cultural differences, including what is expected of the instructor and the participant.

Determine if the audience is familiar with typical workplace training techniques common in the United States and what expectations participants have of the facilitator and of each other. Likewise, check to see what gender or religious issues should be considered.

Previous Experience with Virtual Classrooms

Determine if participants have experienced training in a virtual classroom and offer a brief orientation for participants who have no virtual classroom training experience. The purpose is to ease any anxiety participants might have about using the technology and to clarify the expectations for participants during the live session. Demonstrate features such as polls, chat, and instant feedback, and explain the methodology you will use in the future session. Practice with simple introductory poll exercises, such as the type of transportation used to commute or their last vacation trip. Answer participants' questions, and remind them if they need to complete prerequisites before the day of the training.

If participants are not available for a precourse session, prepare and send a recording of an orientation session that demonstrates key features or a document that includes screen shots for the training and explanatory notes and tips.

Environment

Investigate the learners' physical environment (including the availability of computers, telephones, and headsets) in advance of the virtual training to allow time to mitigate any potential disruptive issues. For example, if participants are joining the session from an open office environment and plan to use a microphone and headset, make sure that nonparticipating coworkers and managers understand that the learners are involved in a company-sponsored training event. And, double-check with the remote site IT personnel to ensure enough bandwidth is available for the virtual training session you've designed (i.e., the use of video or other bandwidth draining features incorporated into the design).

Logistics

Training in the global virtual classroom means you leave behind some of the traditional logistical worries associated with traveling long distances and obtaining visas to get to your destination. However, a new set of logistical concerns arises from coordinating different work weeks, public and religious holidays, and time zones.

Workweek and Public Holidays

In many countries including the United States, Brazil, and China, the typical workweek is Monday through Friday. However, in countries such as Egypt, Bangladesh and Saudi Arabia, the work week is Sunday through Thursday. So, first make sure the day(s) you plan to hold your virtual training event matches the workweek where the participants will take the training. Next, check for public and religious holidays, and related dates when most people in the target countries typically take vacations. For example, scheduling a training event in the United States on Thanksgiving or the day after would pretty much guaran-

---

RESOURCES TO HELP WITH GLOBAL LOGISTICS

Time and Date
timeanddate.com/
World Time Server
www.worldtimeserver.com/
Worldwide Daylight Saving
www.webexhibits.org/daylightsaving/g.html
Worldwide Public Holidays
qppstudio.net
Workweek
en.wikipedia.org/wiki/Workweek
Mobile Apps
In addition to web resources, check the app store on your mobile device. Business apps such as global time and date and global holidays are examples of helpful resources.

tee that no one would attend your virtual training event. Other countries have similarly important national holidays, so avoid scheduling these holidays for virtual training.

Time Zones

After you've identified the appropriate date(s) for your training, focus on selecting what time to offer your training. The easiest way ensure you select the right time is to follow a two-step process: (1) Create a ranking of target locations based on proximity to your own time zone and (2) Group the target locations based on similarity of time zone differences.

Then, after determining the location of each participant by country, create a ranking table, based on the proximity to your time zone as shown in Table 8-1.

Now do some research (either through an Internet search or conversations with local colleagues and associates) to make sure you understand the typical business hours for participants and whether any hours of the days should be avoided due to observance of religious practices or typical lunch times. With this information, you can create an acceptable range of time slots for training in multiple countries. Keep in mind both the start and end times of the virtual training event since special transportation or safety concerns might prevent participants from attending if the training ends after business hours.

The time selection becomes more complicated as the number of countries increases. Table 8-1 shows why it may be necessary to repeat a session twice so

Table 8-1 Sample Ranking of Target Locations Based on Proximity to Time Zone of Facilitation Team

City, Country	Time Difference from New York-Based Facilitation Team
São Paulo, Brazil	1 hour ahead
Cairo, Egypt	6 hours ahead
Paris, France	6 hours ahead
New Delhi, India	9.5 hours ahead
Hong Kong	12 hours ahead

that all time zones are accommodated. Note that Brazil, Egypt, and France can be grouped together for the first session, while India and Hong Kong can be grouped together for the second session. Refer to Table 8-2 for an example of start and end times for the two sessions.

If you are delivering multiple sessions sequentially, the logistics will need some careful thought. For example, in Table 8-2, Session 1 takes place during business hours for the facilitation team. However, since the facilitation team must work past regular business hours for Session 2, consider scheduling this session after Session 1 to allow time for the facilitators to rest. Furthermore, if the facilitation team is colocated in New York and the members deliver Session 1 together from the same location, it may be possible to deliver Session 2 from their homes at night since they have already practiced together.

Table 8-2 Example of Start and End Times for Two Sessions with Global Participants

	Start Time	End Time
Session 1		
Facilitation Team: New York	9:00 AM	11:00 AM
Sao Paolo, Brazil	10:00 AM	12:00 PM
Cairo, Egypt	3:00 PM	5:00 PM
Paris, France	3:00 PM	5:00 PM
Session 2		
Facilitation Team: New York	11:00 PM	1:00 AM
New Delhi, India	8:30 AM (next day)	10:30 AM
Hong Kong	11:00 AM (next day)	1:00 PM

Daylight Saving Time

Daylight saving time (DST) in the United States (with the exception of Arizona and Hawaii) starts on the second Sunday in March and ends on the first Sunday in November. Member countries of the European Union observe European

---

TIP

Ensure that the start and end times you advertise have taken into account daylight saving time differences; otherwise, you may show up an hour early or late for your session.

Summer Time from the last Sunday in March to the last Sunday in October. A number of countries, such as Argentina, China, India, and Japan, don't observe DST, while other countries follow a completely different set of rules. For example, Brazil observes DST between the third Sunday in October and the third Sunday in February. If your sessions will take place during the Fall or Spring, double-check your time zone conversions to ensure you have accounted for DST differences among countries.

See Table 8-3 for an example of how to make course adjustments based on the five key areas just covered. As you can see, these adjustments are minor. However, such small adjustments make a big difference for global participants.

SKILLS OF THE GLOBAL VIRTUAL FACILITATOR

The global virtual classroom facilitator has skills that span many areas in addition to general facilitation skills and subject matter expertise as described below.

Cultural and Language Skills

Geert Hofstede, the founder of comparative intercultural research theory, says that culture is the "collective programming of the mind that distinguishes the members of one category of people from another." Edward T. Hall, another researcher in the field of cross-cultural communication, explains cultural differences this way: "Culture hides much more than it reveals, and strangely enough what it hides, it hides most effectively from its own participants."

Our native culture impacts how we communicate with others, how we work together cooperatively and collaboratively, and informs the assumptions we make about others. That's why a deep understanding of our own cultural assumptions is important for global facilitators. For example, if you were raised,

Table 8-3 Examples of Global Learner Needs and Course Adjustments

Learner Needs	Course Adjustment
1. **Language**: Common language for participants is English, and it is everyone's second language.	• Simplify the language in your materials. • Provide all materials in advance so participants have time to review and check for unfamiliar vocabulary. • Slow the pace of your facilitation.
2. **Cultural Differences**: Participants come from collectivist cultures with an aversion to risk taking and standing out.	• Learn as much as you can about participants by speaking to managers, HR staff, or people who grew up in the target countries. • Design the session to include a variety of activities, including small group work.
3. **Experience with Virtual Classroom**: This will be the first time participants attend virtual classroom training.	• Offer a precourse orientation session. • Describe expectations regarding participation.
4. **Environment**: In two locations, participants are in an open floor arrangement. In other locations, participants are in cubicles or offices.	• Contact managers to let them know that participants will be doing training with a headset or find conference rooms for participants to use during the session.
5. **Logistics**: Participants are based in five different time zones with 1–12 hour time differences from the facilitation team.	• Break participants into two groups based on location and deliver the session twice to accommodate time zone differences.

educated, and work in the United States, some of your cultural assumptions may include the following:

- Speaking directly and openly is best.
- Praising an individual is a good way to encourage someone.
- The importance of individual freedom to choose your own way and accept the consequences of those choices.

But, in other parts of the world, participants may assume that:

- It's wrong to ask questions of an instructor.
- Being singled out and praised is bad.
- The value of the common greater good is more important than valuing one's own needs.

Culturally self-aware facilitators understand that their cultural assumptions are their own and that participants from other cultures have their own cultural assumptions.

Pace

If you learned to speak a second language as an adult, you likely recall how difficult it was to understand a native speaker of the language talking at a full conversational pace in person. Understanding a phone conversation is even more difficult because the body language and lip-reading queues are absent.

As a facilitator, you can help the nonnative speakers of your language by slowing down the pace of your speech to give them more time to process your words.

TIP

Practice the pronunciation of participant names in advance. Even if your pronunciation is not perfect, participants will appreciate your effort.

International English

A skilled facilitator also uses "international" English, meaning English that is free from country-specific idioms ("keep your nose to the grindstone" or "put your ducks in a row"), colloquialisms ("I need my coffee fix" or "beats me"), or slang expressions ("ya'll" or "my bad"). Of course, some American slang and other expressions have become international, so the best advice is to check with your contacts in target countries for clarification. The same rule of "internationalizing" your language applies if the session is being delivered in German, Arabic, or another language.

For example, instead of asking the participant to play "devil's advocate," you would ask the participant to "offer another perspective." Instead of thanking the learner for going the "extra mile," thank the participant for the "extra effort." Or, instead of complimenting a participant by saying they "hit a home run," say that the "response was excellent."

TIP

Dr. Andrea Edmundson, CPLP, Global Learning Strategist for eWorld Learning, Inc.

When you facilitate training for global audiences, you need to become more conscious of your speech. To do this, I recommend these steps: (1) Think about what you are going to say and say it naturally first. (2) Record yourself, or write down what you plan to say. (3) Do an audit of your words, and determine where you can simplify the structure of your sentences, remove idioms, colloquialisms and verb phrases (e.g., look over, make up, filter out).

Once you have transcribed your words, the Spelling and Grammar feature in Microsoft Word can help you conduct the audit by setting stringent standards. With Word open, go to the File tab and select "Options" and then "Proofing." In the Proofing section, under "When correcting spelling and grammar" section, make sure that all boxes are checked and that the Writing Style is set to "Grammar & Style." Once you have selected "Grammar & Style," click on the "Settings" button and check ALL of the boxes! Save your changes. Now, whenever you conduct a Spelling & Grammar check, Word will use rules that help the nonnative English speaker. In addition, at the end, you'll see a pop up box with readability statistics, including an approximate reading grade level of your writing. Your sentences should average 20 words in length, with 3 to 6 sentences per paragraph. In addition, you should strive for a reading grade level of nine or 10 for a nonnative speaker. If the grade level is too high, review your language to see where you can simplify the text.

ADJUSTING CONTENT AND EXERCISES

An exciting aspect of a global audience is the diversity in the virtual classroom. People raised and educated in different parts of the world will come to your virtual classroom with a variety of learning styles and perceptions about what is expected of the facilitator and the participant. Hopefully, you've gained valuable knowledge and audience expectations based on your participant analysis as described earlier. Then match diversity with diversity by offering participants a variety of exercises and giving them options for responding, such as typing in chat or verbalizing on the phone. Participants will select what feels right for them. Use polls and instant feedback tools to engage participants and overcome shyness around speaking or typing in a nonnative language.

Often, virtual classroom participants come from multiple countries. Furthermore, a participant from one part of the world may have been educated, lived, and/or worked in another part of the world, so it's difficult to make assumptions about cultural tendencies. There is no magical solution for addressing culturally diverse learning styles. What *is* important is the facilitator's awareness of cultural differences and the incorporation of a range of activities to meet the diverse needs of a global audience.

You can also set expectations with clear instructions about how participants will benefit from the session and the types of exercises offered. You can incorporate this content through precourse orientation as described earlier, by speaking individually with participants, or by asking a local counterpart to convey these messages for you.

Making adjustments to your content will improve your virtual classroom training with global participants. What follows are a few areas to consider.

Presentation Slides and Exercises

All participants, even those from other countries, expect to see content that makes sense to them, as well as examples they understand. Carefully review your course materials (including all support material, such as slides and handouts) to remove or adjust culturally inappropriate content, examples, and images. Remove references to sports, politics, and entertainment, such as popular national television shows, performers, or any other limited pop culture references. If your slides include images of people, make sure nothing about the images might be offensive to your own careful sensibilities and then ask someone familiar with the target culture to advise you on the image's use.

For exercises and interactivity, your global participants need verbal and written instructions. Add slides with brief instructions to clearly describe what is expected. Tell participants how the exercise will work, how long it will last, which interactive features they are expected to use, and any materials they need to complete an exercise.

Simplified Text

Simplify slide text to make it easier for nonnative speakers to understand the content. Simplified means that you make the text concise, ensuring every word on the slide is necessary to convey the concept. Simple text will also help your nonnative speaker participants to review concepts by looking up key words in a dictionary or online translation tool when needed.

Translation

If course materials will be translated into one or more languages, concise and precise terminology will yield more accurate translations. Once translated, ask a native speaker familiar with the content or concepts presented to review the content. Keep in mind that language meaning and usage varies among countries. For example, using a Mexico City-based translation firm to translate materials into Spanish for a course being taught in Spain would not be the optimal translation option. Furthermore, if participants share a common language but

---

TIP

Dr. Andrea Edmundson, CPLP, Global Learning Strategist for eWorld Learning, Inc.

Sometimes you can recognize symptoms that there are cultural issues in your virtual classroom with global participants. For example, if audience members are reluctant to participate, they may be intimidated by an exercise that is unfamiliar to them. In this case, give them more instructions and more time to complete the exercise.

Some virtual classroom tools allow you to run a quiz in real time, and you may find that the audience is reluctant to respond. For people from a culture with high *uncertainty avoidance,* you may need to preface the quiz by telling people that mistakes are okay and that the results won't count against them. Always try to see your training from the learner's perspective to diagnose cultural issues.

Josebe Bilbao-Henry, Language & Culture Program Manager, The World Bank

Do as much research as you can about your global participants before delivering training in a virtual classroom. Think about potential cultural reactions people may have to your training. One tool that helps me is the Culture GPS app, based on Geert Hofstede's cultural dimensions. For example, let's say I'll be delivering training to participants in Bhutan. The tool shows that Bhutan has a high power distance rating. That means that they see the facilitator as an authority figure. For this session, I should not downplay my authority—I should clearly explain my credentials. I would also inform them ahead of time that I will be calling on individuals from time to time to answer a question and that it is not meant to intimidate, but only to get everyone to participate.

The best way to handle potential cultural issues is to address them before your session or at the beginning of the session. You can send instructions to participants before the session begins to explain that there will be participatory activities. You can also include a slide at the beginning of your session describing how the session will work. You may want to explain that some activities may feel more natural for them while others may not, but there will be a variety of activities and they are expected to participate in all of them.

Your goal should be to make sure people feel comfortable doing activities so they maximize their learning. Doing a little bit of preparation can help you reach this goal.

come from different countries, ensure that the translation represents an "international" version of the language, rather than a country-specific version of the language.

ADJUSTING THE USE OF VIRTUAL CLASSROOM FEATURES FOR GLOBAL PARTICIPANTS

Maximize learning transfer and create a positive learning experience for global participants by making small adjustments in the way you use virtual classroom features. Here are some suggestions.

> **TIP**
>
> If your session will be conducted in a language other than English, check the language settings of your virtual classroom tool. Some tools allow you to change the language for the user interface.

Chat

Global audiences benefit from a well-utilized chat area, where chat is used to support verbal comments. To do this, simply ask the producer to type key messages and summaries into the chat area to emphasize points as the facilitator speaks. Nonnative speakers benefit from this written confirmation of their understanding. To make this process run smoothly, prepare a text file with the key messages in advance. Then the producer only has to cut and paste these messages into the chat area as the facilitator speaks. Native speakers will also benefit from this practice!

Polling

Polls engage participants and overcome nonnative speaker shyness about speaking or typing in a nonnative language. Let participants know that their responses are anonymous if that is the case for your virtual classroom tool. Make sure that the question-and-answer set for the poll is concise and easy to understand. Give an international audience extra time to answer.

Video

Provide a transcript of any video provided in the training so nonnative speakers can follow along using the written transcript. The transcript helps with comprehension and gives these participants a tool for later reference.

Breakout Rooms

Some participants are uncomfortable with large group exercises and prefer collaborative, small group work. Consider using breakout rooms for small group work to complement large group activities and individual exercises to add variety to your session.

If possible, divide participants by language so that they can discuss in their native language, if appropriate. If the common language of the session is English and you expect participants to share their work from the breakout room, ask the groups to take notes in English.

REHEARSING

One of the easiest ways to identify and correct unsuitable content in a global training program is to rehearse the session with a mock audience. Include participants from the target country(ies), and instruct them to listen and look for anything culturally inappropriate or difficult for a global audience to understand. If your mock audience identifies problem areas, ask for suggestions or brainstorm ideas on how to adjust and improve the materials. If you can't rehearse with someone from the target country, look for someone who has experience living or working in the target country. As a last resort, rehearse with someone who did not grow up in the same country as you. This person may be able to spot the most egregious errors.

Ask the mock audience members to provide feedback using a tool such as the "Rehearsal Feedback Form" in Appendix G. Try to get specific feedback and examples from the mock audience on areas that might pose problems for a global audience, so that you can make specific adjustments to your training. Finally, ask mock audience members for feedback on Internet connectivity/response times of the virtual classroom tools, especially if you plan to show a video or use a webcam.

TIP

As you deliver training to global audiences, identify participants who can become informal advisers to you and can serve as cultural mentors for future training.

CONCLUSION

Facilitating a session with global participants requires research, empathy, and creativity. Put yourself in your participant's shoes. Then, think of yourself as a cultural anthropologist and try to understand how your participants will experience training in the virtual classroom. By considering the participants' perspectives and making adjustments, participants will feel included regardless of their location or cultural background and your session will run more smoothly.

Table 8-4 includes a checklist of important areas to consider for your next session.

Table 8-4 Global Virtual Classroom Planning and Preparation Form

Topic	Action	My Notes
1. Logistics	Select a date and time that is convenient for participants.	
2. Environment	Find out if participants have access to proper equipment. Check with IT about bandwidth constraints.	
3. Language	Select language(s); if English, use neutral English and adjust your pace.	
4. Images	Select culturally appropriate images.	
5. Learning Styles	Select exercises that align with the culture of the audience.	
6. Rehearsal	Rehearse with someone from the target country.	
7. Virtual Classroom Features	Adjust virtual classroom feature use for a global audience.	
8. Learner Support	Use chat to reiterate key learning points as the facilitator speaks.	

CONTINUOUS LEARNING

1. Find a coworker, neighbor, or friend who was born in a different country from you. Ask about her culture, traditions, and differences between her country and the United States.
2. Locate local ethnic/cultural groups, and visit a festival or other event that they sponsor.
3. Read books about cross-cultural communications (e.g., *When Cultures Collide, Culture Savvy*).
4. Read newspapers and magazines whose perspective comes from outside the United States (e.g., *International Herald Tribune, The Times of India, The Daily Telegraph (UK), China Daily*). Compare and contrast the perspectives that different newspapers bring to the same news story.
5. Take a virtual field trip to another country with your facilitation team. Pick one country a month and read about the country's history, geography, and culture.
6. Study another language.

References

Christopher, Darlene. "Facilitating in the Global Virtual Classroom." *ASTD Infoline*. Alexandria, VA: ASTD Press, 2011.

Christopher, Darlene. "Harder Focus on the Global Classroom." *T&D Magazine*. February 2011, 30–31.

Hall, Edward T., "Culture Is Communication," In *Basic Concepts of Intercultural Communication: Selected Readings*, edited by Milton J. Bennett, pages 53–67. Yarmouth, ME: Intercultural Press, 1998.

McClay, Renie and LuAnn Irwin. *The Essential Guide to Training Global Audiences*. San Francisco: Pfeiffer, 2008.

Edmundson, Andrea. "Culturally Accessible E-Learning: An Overdue Global Business Imperative." *T&D Magazine*. April 2009.

Edmundson, Andrea. "Training for Multiple Cultures." *ASTD Infoline*. Alexandria, VA: ASTD Press, 2010.

Hofstede, Geert and Gert Jan Hofstede. "Culture." Retrieved on October 30, 2013, http://www.geerthofstede.com/culture.

American Society for Training and Development (ASTD). *Learning's Role in Globally Dispersed Workforces: An ASTD Research Study*. Alexandria, VA: ASTD Press, 2008.

Lewis, Richard D. *When Cultures Collide*. Boston, MA: Nicholas Brealey International, 2006.

Vorhauser-Smith, Sylvia. "Lost in Translation." *Talent Management Magazine*. May 2012, 24–26.

NINE

Ideas for Icebreakers and Exercises

Maintaining a high level of interactivity with participants is essential to executing a successful virtual classroom session. In my experience, well-designed interactivity that makes the most of the full range of features of the virtual classroom leads to engaging training with high learning transfer. Chapter 5, "Developing Virtual Classroom Training," covered design in the virtual classroom; this chapter provides specific examples of icebreakers and exercises to incorporate into your design.

The ideas in this chapter range from simple to complex interactions. Some of the ideas include specific examples, so as you read think creatively about your content—with a few small adjustments to these ideas you can tweak them to meet your needs.

Each example starts with an overview and objective to give you the big picture. Some examples work with any size audience, while others are designed for small classes of up to 20 participants. Each example suggests what to include in the content sharing area, along with which features are used for the icebreaker or exercise: chat, drawing tools, instant feedback, or polls. Then follow the instructions for a step-by-step process and review the cultural considerations and tips for extra ideas.

ICEBREAKERS

Kicking off a training session with an icebreaker helps to get participants warmed up and ready to learn. Icebreakers in the virtual classroom serve the dual purpose of energizing participants and ensuring they are comfortable with the interactive tools in the classroom.

Just like every other aspect of training in the virtual classroom, icebreakers require planning and preparation. For more ideas on icebreakers, including instructions and preparation needed, read through the following ideas.

Just Three Words

Overview: A simple game to use as an icebreaker or energizer where participants have fun typing three-word phrases into chat.

Objective: To warm up participants and give them experience using the chat feature.

Audience Size: Any

Content Area: A slide with the text "Just Three Words" and the instructions "Warm-up: Type any three-word phrase into chat."

Features Used: ☑ Chat   ☐ Drawing Tools   ☐ Instant Feedback   ☐ Poll

Preparation: Load slide into content area and open chat area.

Duration: 1 to 5 minutes

Process:

1. Explain to participants that they should type a three-word phrase into the chat area. The phrase can be about anything that comes to mind.
2. Model the activity by typing in three words (for example: I like dogs, or Where's my coffee?).
3. Let this exercise run for a minute or two, commenting on some of the responses and encouraging participants to post more than one response.

Cultural Considerations: If participants are hesitant to post in the chat, remind them that there is no right or wrong answer in this exercise.

Tips:

- If you ask participants to log in to your session early, run this icebreaker as people join. Leave the slide with instructions on the screen so people understand what is going on in the chat as they join the class.
- Position this as a fun exercise where participants have free reign to type whatever comes to mind.
- Getting participants active in chat with this exercise at the beginning of your session will help encourage the use of chat throughout a session.

Would You Rather. . . .

Overview: A simple warm-up game to use as an icebreaker or energizer where participants respond to humorous poll questions.

Objective: To warm up participants and give them experience with the poll feature.

Audience Size: Any

Content Area: A slide with the text "Would You Rather. . . ."

Features Used: ☐ Chat   ☐ Drawing Tools   ☐ Instant Feedback   ☑ Poll

Preparation: Load slide into content area. Prepare a few polls that include the question, "Would You Rather. . . .?" The answer is a choice of two-item sets, such as:

- Have a beach holiday?/Have a mountain holiday?
- Be invisible?/Be able to read minds?
- Lose your wallet?/Lose your mobile phone?
- Be stranded on a deserted island alone?/Be stranded on a deserted island with someone you don't like?
- See the future?/Change the past?
- Be a dog?/Be a cat?

Duration: 1 to 2 minutes

Process:

1. Explain to participants that they should answer the poll question(s).
2. Post poll questions simultaneously or sequentially and share tallied results with the audience after the majority of participants have responded.

Cultural Considerations: Remind participants that there is no right or wrong answer and responses are anonymous.

Tips:

- If you ask participants to sign into your session early, run this icebreaker as people join. As people log in to the class, encourage them to vote.
- Getting participants used to responding to polls in this exercise at the beginning of your session will help encourage poll responses throughout a session.

Interaction Warm Up

Overview: This warm-up exercise serves the dual purpose of providing an ice-breaker and an overview of the interactive features.

Objective: To introduce participants to the interactive features of the virtual classroom early in a session and set the tone for a high level of interactivity.

Audience Size: Any

Content Area: Prepare a set of slides with this text and images to illustrate key concepts or screen shots of virtual classroom features: Slide #1, "Interacting in the Virtual Classroom"; slide #2, "Let's Answer a Poll Question"; slide #3, "Let's Chat"; slide #4, "Instant Feedback"; and slide #5, "Whiteboard Practice."

Features Used: ☑ Chat   ☑ Drawing Tools   ☑ Instant Feedback   ☑ Poll

Preparation: Load slides with simple instructions and screen shots to support the selected interactions. Load a poll in advance. Prepare a Word document or text file with a question that you can copy and paste into chat. Prepare a whiteboard with labeled quadrants.

Duration: 5 to 10 minutes

Process:

1. **Opening slide (slide #1)**: After welcoming participants and making introductions, show a slide with the text "Interacting in the Virtual Classroom."

2. **Post a poll (slide #2)**: Let participants know if their poll responses are anonymous or not. Post an introductory poll with an "easy" question that relates to your content. For example: "How many years of experience do you have with X?" or "How many years have you worked in X or as X?" When all responses have been collected, publish the results for all to see, comment on the results, thank the participants for their responses, and move on to the next interaction.

3. **Chat (slide #3)**: Copy and paste a predetermined chat question from a Word document. For example: "Where are you today? Type the city

and state or province." Or, "How many employees do you supervise? Type the number." Comment verbally about some (not all) of the responses. If you have a second person helping produce your session, he may also respond to or comment on the responses via chat.

4. **Instant feedback (slide #4)**: Tell participants that they can also communicate with you during the session by using the instant feedback feature (the name of this feature will vary depending on your tool). Show a slide with screen shots of the icon status change so you can demonstrate where it is located on the screen and how to enable it. Then ask participants to respond to a question by changing their status. For example: "Raise your hand if the audio is clear." Or, "Change your status to *agree* if you supervise remote employees. Change your status to *disagree* if you do not supervise remote employees." Comment on the results, thank the participants, reset everyone's status to neutral, and then move on.

5. **Whiteboard (slide #5)**: Draw a simple quadrant with labels or show an image of a quadrant with labels. Ask participants to use their pointer tool to indicate the box that is the best match. If your tool doesn't have pointers for participants, ask them to select a box and write their name on the screen. For example, you might ask: "Which region of the world do you support in your work?" Then show a quadrant labeled Americas, Europe, Asia, Middle East. Participants will then fill in the quadrants with their names. Comment on the responses and segue into your next topic.

Cultural Considerations: By practicing using the features at the beginning of the session, you are giving participants "permission" to continue using the features throughout the session.

Tips:

- The order of this activity is not as important as making sure you expose participants to the interactive features you plan to use throughout the session.

■ Rehearse these introductory interactions so they are smooth. A flawless first few minutes will set a tone for a professional delivery.

Originally published in Biech, Elaine, editor. *The Book of Road-Tested Activities*. San Francisco, CA: Pfeiffer, 2011, pages 391–393.

Getting to Know You

Overview: Upon introducing themselves to the group, participants share something that the group does not know about them.

Objective: To get participants to introduce themselves to the group and warm up with the drawing tools.

Audience Size: Up to 12

Content Area: A slide with the text, "Introduce Yourself," and the instructions "Write your name at the top of a square, and then draw a picture that illustrates a hobby or interest."

Features Used: ☐ Chat   ☑ Drawing Tools   ☐ Instant Feedback   ☐ Poll

Duration: 5 to 7 minutes

Setup: Prepare a slide or create a grid on a whiteboard with large empty squares equivalent to the number of participants.

Process:

1. **Describe the activity:** Tell participants they will be introducing themselves to the group. Ask participants to "claim" a square by writing their name at the top. Tell them to draw a simple picture that illustrates their hobby using the whiteboard drawing tools. The rest of the group will guess what they drew.

2. **Participant introductions:** When everyone is done drawing, ask the person in the top left square to introduce himself or herself by saying his/her name and office location. Then ask participants to guess the person's hobby based on the drawing they see. Continue until all participants have introduced themselves.

Tip: This activity works best with small groups and classes with a long duration. For a larger class (12+ participants), adjust this activity by preparing a slide with participant photos and names. Start at the top right of the slide and ask participants to introduce themselves verbally and tell the group a hobby or interest.

EXERCISES

Weaving interactive exercises into a training session encourages learners to participate actively in the learning process rather than just be a spectator. Interactive exercises give participants a chance to enhance their understanding of a topic by analyzing, applying, and internalizing new information. The following section offers a variety of ideas to engage participants with the core content of a session.

Guess the Word

Overview: Participants try to guess a word that illustrates a key concept from course material.

Objective: To review and discuss a key concept(s) to wrap up a session.

Audience Size: Up to 20

Content Areas: Prepare a slide(s) with blank spaces representing the letters of a key concept. Write a clue a clue at the bottom of the screen.

Features Used: ☐ Chat   ☑ Drawing Tools   ☐ Instant Feedback   ☐ Poll

Duration: 5 to 10 minutes

Setup: Think of a word or phrase that illustrates a key concept from your material. Create a slide(s) and load it into the content area.

Process:

1. **Introduce the activity**: Tell participants that they will play a game as a review to wrap up the session.

2. **Start the activity**: Show the slide with blank spaces and tell participants that they will take turns guessing letters of the mystery word on the screen. Start at the top of the participant list, and ask each person to guess a letter. Use the drawing tools to write letters in the spaces when someone guesses a letter correctly. After a few letters have been posted, tell participants they can use their turn to either guess a letter or guess the word or phrase. Continue until a participant guesses the word or phrase correctly.

3. **Debrief**: Remind participants of the importance of the key word or phrase they have just guessed and tie it back into previous learning.

Cultural Considerations: Americans may recognize this game because it's similar to a popular television game show. If you have global participants in the classroom, you may need to spend an extra minute or two explaining the process.

Tip: Select a word or phrase that is long enough to give everyone a chance to play. Or, considering doing multiple rounds of this game by selecting more than one word/phrase to guess.

Cast Your Vote

Overview: By soliciting feedback from participants via polls, the facilitator uses the responses to direct a discussion.

Objective: To validate the participants' experience before starting a discussion.

Audience Size: Any

Content Area: Prepare a slide with text that represents the topic of the poll.

Features Used: ☐ Chat   ☐ Drawing Tools   ☐ Instant Feedback   ☑ Poll

Duration: 5 to 10 minutes

Setup: Load the slide. Create poll questions related to your content. For example, if you are leading a session on how to have a difficult conversation with direct reports, post polls such as: "When having a difficult conversation, do you share the good news or the bad news first?" (Answers: Good news, Bad news) "Do you rehearse a difficult conversation before you have it?" (Answers: Always, Sometimes, Never, Not Applicable).

Process:

1. **Post a poll:** Ask participants to respond to the poll. When everyone has responded, reveal the answers (broadcast the results).

2. **Lead a discussion:** Comment on the results and invite others to comment. Lead a discussion on the poll results, and tie it into your content.

Cultural Considerations: Polls are an easy way to interact with a global audience, especially if you are facilitating in a language that is not the first language of the participants. Remind participants that their responses are anonymous.

Tip: If your tool allows you to hide responses from participants until you choose to reveal them, use that feature. Revealing the responses after everyone has responded will prevent biased answers.

Whiteboard Squares

Overview: The audience participates in an interactive question-and-answer session by writing answers to a question on the whiteboard.

Objective: To engage participants individually in a simultaneous group activity.

Audience Size: Up to 10

Content Area: A grid with squares equal to the number of participants.

Features Used: ☐ Chat ☑ Drawing Tools ☐ Instant Feedback ☐ Poll

Duration: 5 to 10 minutes

Setup: Display the whiteboard with a grid. Enable drawing tools for all participants.

Process:

1. **Claim a square**: Ask participant to write their name at the bottom of a square to claim it using the drawing tools. If two people claim the same square, ask one person to move to an empty square.

2. **Ask a question**: Ask a question out loud and also write it at the top of the whiteboard. Then, ask participants to write the answer in their square using the drawing tools. For example, if you are leading a session on team building, ask: "What skill can you contribute to the team that may not be obvious to the rest of us?" Or, if you are facilitating a class on writing ask: "What one word summarizes your writing style?"

3. **Discuss responses**: Lead a verbal discussion about the responses. Continue with a new question if desired, and ask participants to erase their previous response or open a new whiteboard.

Tip: Make sure everyone knows how to use the drawing tools and the eraser before you start. Also make sure that participant names are legible so it's clear who wrote which response.

Word Scramble

Overview: A closing exercise where participants guess a word that represents a key concept or topic from the session and then describe what they learned about that concept.

Audience Size: Any

Content Area: A set of slides with a jumbled word followed by the word spelled correctly.

Features Used: ☑ Chat   ☐ Drawing Tools   ☐ Instant Feedback   ☐ Poll

Duration: 5 to 10 minutes

Setup: Think of 3 to 5 key concepts from your content. The concepts should be one or two words each. Scramble the words, and put one scrambled concept on a slide, followed by a slide with the word(s) spelled correctly. Repeat this process for all of the key concepts you plan to include.

Process:

1. **Explain the exercise**: Tell participants that you are going to show a slide with a scrambled word that represents a key concept from the session. They should look at the word, try to unscramble it, and type the correct word in chat.
2. **Post the correct word**: When you see a correct response(s) in chat, acknowledge it and move to the next slide to display the unscrambled word.
3. **Ask participants for a key takeaway**: Now ask participants to type in chat a key takeaway or something important that they learned about that concept. Comment on the responses.
4. **Repeat with another scrambled word**: Follow the process above.

Tips:

- If working with participants whose first language isn't English, it may take a few moments longer for participants to unscramble the word(s).
- Turn this into a game by giving points to the first person to unscramble each word and see who wins the most points.

■ This exercise can be done verbally instead of using chat. Ask participants to call out responses and, after the word has been unscrambled, ask participants to take turns telling the class something they learned about the key concept.

Scripted Role Plays for Employee Feedback Conversations

Overview: Participants read a scripted role play out loud and then discuss it.

Objective: To practice giving and receiving feedback for a performance review in a simulated environment.

Audience Size: 10–20

Content Area: A slide with the text "Scripted role play: how to [insert the name of the situation]." For example, the situation could be: "How to Respond to Unclear Feedback." Another slide should contain the text: "Two volunteers needed. Click on "Raise Hand" to volunteer" (you will need to word this slide to match the feature labels used in your virtual classroom tool). A third slide will have the text for the scripted role play.

Features Used: ☐ Chat   ☐ Drawing Tools   ☑ Instant Feedback   ☐ Poll

Duration: 5 to 7 minutes

Setup: Prepared slides loaded in meeting room. Set instant feedback status to neutral.

Process:

1. **Describe the activity**: Post the opening slide with the text "Scripted role play." Tell participants that the activity will be a scripted role play where they will practice how to respond to unclear feedback in a performance review conversation.

2. **Solicit volunteers**: Show next slide with text "Two volunteers needed." Explain that you need two volunteers to read a role play.

3. **Assign roles**: Call on the first two people who raise their hands and assign one person the role of supervisor and the other the role of employee. If you have muted participant phones or microphones, unmute the audio for the two volunteers.

4. **Read out loud**: Show the next slide with a script, and ask the volunteers to read it aloud. The script should be labeled with text for the supervisor and text for the employee. Alternate the text so that each person reads twice. For example:

   Supervisor: "I think you need to improve your interpersonal skills."

   Employee: "Can you give me some suggestions about how I can do that?"

Supervisor: "You could improve in the area of showing respect to other people."

Employee: "I feel like I do respect other people. What can I do to let people know that? What suggestions do you have for me?"

Supervisor: "In meetings, you appear disinterested when someone else is speaking. If you pay attention to the speaker or make a comment, it is a sign of respect."

5. **Debrief**: Ask participants: "What are the key learning points?" "What else can you include in this conversation?" "How does this fit with your experience with performance conversations?"

Cultural Considerations: This exercise should be done without the participants' managers in the room. Otherwise, some participants may feel uncomfortable. Check with local managers and human resources staff to develop a script that is appropriate for your audience.

Tips:

- Without the visual clues and body language of a face-to-face setting, it's difficult to carry out a traditional role play exercise in a virtual classroom. However, scripting the role play provides a starting point. Often, participants who are reading the script will continue the role play on their own, but the script helps to get them started.

- Virtual classroom participants need clear, deliberate instructions. Describe exactly what you want participants to do verbally and use a slide to support your instructions (e.g., raise your hand, read out loud, etc.)

Originally published in Biech, Elaine, editor. *The Book of Road-Tested Activities*. San Francisco, CA: Pfeiffer, 2011, pages 397–399.

Partner Chat (for Adobe Connect)

Overview: In a traditional classroom, trainers often ask participants to discuss a topic with a partner or in a small group. You can replicate this exercise in the virtual classroom using the chat feature. With Adobe Connect, you can post multiple chat pods on the screen. Prior to posting the pods, use the "rename" function to rename the chat pod with the chat partner names. Post a question on the screen for participants to discuss, and then watch the screen explode with activity.

Objectives: To encourage small group interaction on a topic.

Audience Size: Up to 16

Content Area: Slide with instructions.

Features Used: ☑ Chat   ☐ Drawing Tools   ☐ Instant Feedback   ☐ Poll

Duration: 5 to 10 minutes

Setup: Create a new layout with a slide with instructions at the top of the screen: Chat with your partners for 4 minutes by answering this question (insert a question). Then create multiple chat pods placed on the main part of the screen. Put participants into groups of 2 to 4 and use the "rename" function to rename each chat pod with the names of the participant who are part of the group.

Process:

1. **Describe the activity**: Tell participants that they will be discussing a question with their chat partner(s). Read the question out loud (for example, "What was your biggest take away from this morning's session?" or "Which of the five steps will be the most challenging to implement?")

2. **Start the activity**: Tell participants to look for their name in the label of the chat pod and begin posting responses to the question. Tell participants they have 4 minutes to chat with their partner(s).

3. **Stop and debrief**: When time is up, tell participants to stop chatting. Call on a few people by name and ask them to share insights from their chat comments.

Cultural Considerations: In some cultures, participants may not be comfortable working in pairs with some who is senior in rank.

Tips:

- Include the instructions on a slide that is visible throughout the exercise, especially if participants are responding to more than one question.
- If you are using a tool that doesn't allow for multiple chat areas, assign chat partners and tell participants to send private chat messages. When time is up ask a few people to volunteer and share some of their chat discussion verbally with the group.

OTHER SIMPLE WAYS TO ADD INTERACTIVITY

Discuss a Picture

Display a picture that illustrates a concept you are teaching. Ask the audience to call out or type in chat what they observe in the picture. You can do this as an icebreaker by showing an image of an optical illusion and then asking or polling people on what they observe.

Prioritize a List

Focus the group on identifying their priorities by asking them to call out items while you make a list on the whiteboard. For example, ask: "What are the qualities of a good mentor?" Once you've gathered the typed list of qualities, copy and paste them into a poll and ask participants to vote on the top three qualities that make a good mentor. Your poll results will reveal the most important qualities, as prioritized by the group. Use the poll results as the basis of a discussion.

Scavenger Hunt

If your participants need to know how to access information on a website or how to use an application, place questions about the website on the screen, such as a poll question, and a question to respond to via chat. Then ask them to open a new browser and go to the site to search for the answers to the questions.

Chat Takeaway Goal

As you conclude your session, ask participants what they will do differently as a result of the session. Ask them to type a response in chat. Tell participants you will email them their text response in two weeks (or whatever length of time is appropriate) as a reminder.

CONTINUOUS LEARNING

1. Brainstorm a list of icebreakers or exercises you have either led as an instructor or participated in as a learner in a traditional classroom and think of how you can convert to a virtual classroom delivery.

2. For more ideas on activities to include in your virtual classroom, get a book like *The Book of Road Tested Activities* or visit Thiagi's Training Games site (http://www.thiagi.com/games.html), and look for activities that you can convert to virtual classroom delivery.

TEN

Additional Uses for the Virtual Classroom

HERE'S HOW TO:

- Use the virtual classroom for knowledge sharing.
- Use the virtual classroom to support a community of practice.
- Understand the challenges presented by the use of mobile technology.

Clearly, the tools available for the virtual classroom offer powerful and versatile features that can be used by training professionals in creative ways to build engaging and effective learning events. This chapter offers substantial case studies that demonstrate how some of these features were used by well-known organizations to drive innovation and support knowledge exchange in a community of practice. Finally, learn more about how to incorporate participants who join a virtual classroom using a mobile device.

USING THE VIRTUAL CLASSROOM FOR KNOWLEDGE SHARING

Reported by Charles Gluck, Instructional Innovator and Dan Bliton, Instructional Strategist, Booz Allen Hamilton

We develop innovation and knowledge sharing events for Booz Allen Hamilton called TurboFests. TurboFests use the Adobe Connect platform to support the 1,400 person "Training, Education, and Systems Support" community of practice in the firm. Each TurboFest contains a series of Turbo Presentations. Each virtual presentation uses a 20×20 format (called a PechaKucha format) that allows presenters exactly 20 seconds to comment on each of the 20 slides in the Turbo Presentation. Presenters submit applications to speak on a variety of innovative topics that are meant to showcase new ideas, information, and best practices. Topics have included how to work and lead in virtual environments, design thinking, and cognitive apprenticeship.

The Turbo Presentations are meant to address the need for organizations to find cost-effective ways to develop employees' competencies through smart management. In particular, these events help Booz Allen speakers present relevant information in a structured and engaging way. The need to communicate effectively is a key competency for Booz Allen employees both person and virtually. Presenting at a TurboFest is a great stretch activity that quickly expands speaking skills. Another benefit of a TurboFest is that it appeals to both extroverts, who have a story to tell, and introverts, who appreciate the structured format and/or prefer public speaking to a virtual audience instead of an in-person audience.

TurboFests are one-hour events that happen once a year. Anyone in the firm can apply to present and a panel selects the top nine entries who train for the event over a three-month period. Speakers attend four one-hour training virtual classroom sessions to learn about presenting in the virtual platform using Adobe Connect. The presenters also learn best practices for visual story telling, including how to develop good visuals and how to draw participants into the session with a combination of message/data and a narrative story line.

Presenters are assigned a mentor, a previous TurboFest presenter, who participates in the training sessions and works with presenters throughout the process to help refine key messages and gently guide in the application of best practices. This mentoring activity is part of the collaborative culture at Booz Allen, and it's this focus that helps sustain the culture of mentorship.

Presenters are provided an Adobe Presenter template that automatically advances to the next slide every 20 seconds. The presenters create their presentations so that their comments align with this automatic slide transition. Presenters are also given a link to an Adobe Connect practice room. About one week ahead of the TurboFest, the presenters conduct a dry run to make sure everything is working properly. It usually takes a TurboFest presenters about forty hours to prepare for their presentation.

During the TurboFests, nine presentations are delivered back to back. Chat is active during each presentation, and since the presenter is focused on giving a presentation, the audience is posing and answering questions in a peer-to-peer fashion. Often friends or colleagues who are familiar with a project are online and answer some of the questions.

About 100 to 200 people attend each TurboFest, including senior management. Over the years, TurboFest has become an incubator for new ideas in the organization. The event is also an opportunity for anyone at any level in the organization to spread his or her ideas with a large audience. For example, Charles Gluck did a presentation on cognitive apprenticeship. A human capital specialist colleague heard the presentation and realized that the topic had direct relevance for his work on leadership development. Charles and the human capital specialist collaborated and built a new product. The colleagues eventually published an article on their work in the *International Journal of Training and Development*.

USING THE VIRTUAL CLASSROOM TO SUPPORT A COMMUNITY OF PRACTICE

Reported by Lucy Bassett, Social Protection Specialist, The World Bank

I manage a community of practice for community-based nutrition programs in Central America. We improve the design, implementation, and monitoring and evaluation of these programs. At a conference in October 2011, a potential solution to an important topic (how to motivate community workers) emerged that needed further discussion. Unfortunately, no time was scheduled to continue these discussions.

Since it was not practical to bring conference participants together again in person, we decided to explore a virtual classroom solution. Using a virtual classroom made sense for us because we needed to reach an audience dispersed across several countries, and the solution needed to be convenient and cost effective.

The process we used to prepare for the virtual session was the following:

1. We located a subject matter expert within the community of practice.
2. After learning how to use the virtual classroom tool, we developed the presentation and accompanying interactive exercises with the presenter.
3. We conducted a rehearsal and sent detailed instructions to participants explaining how to join the session and instructions on how to participate in a virtual classroom.

Approximately 30 participants from five countries attended the session, which was facilitated from Washington, DC. The subject matter expert was based in Guatemala. To collect feedback on the pilot session, we sent an online evaluation link to all attendees and asked them to rate different aspects of the session (ease of access, content presented, etc.), as well as offer suggestions for future topics.

Since the initial session, we have conducted additional sessions that continue the dialogue among the community of practice participants using virtual classroom techniques and other modalities, including video conferencing and conference calls.

UNDERSTAND THE CHALLENGES PRESENTED BY THE USE OF MOBILE TECHNOLOGY

Joining a virtual classroom session from a mobile device such as a Smartphone or tablet device offers unprecedented flexibility for training. Participants who are running late for a session can join from their mobile device while in transit and then rejoin once they have access to a computer. It also means that participants who simply cannot get to a computer can participate from a mobile device, while others attend the same session from their computer. Since the features of the virtual classroom are limited on a mobile device, this option only makes sense for a simple virtual classroom session that doesn't include complex interactions, such as breakout rooms and whiteboarding exercises. In other words, including mobile participants will work some, but not all, of the time.

Most virtual classroom tools indicate whether a person is attending from a mobile device or not, as illustrated in Figure 10-1, where two participants have joined using a mobile device which is noted by small rectangle icon to the left of their name.

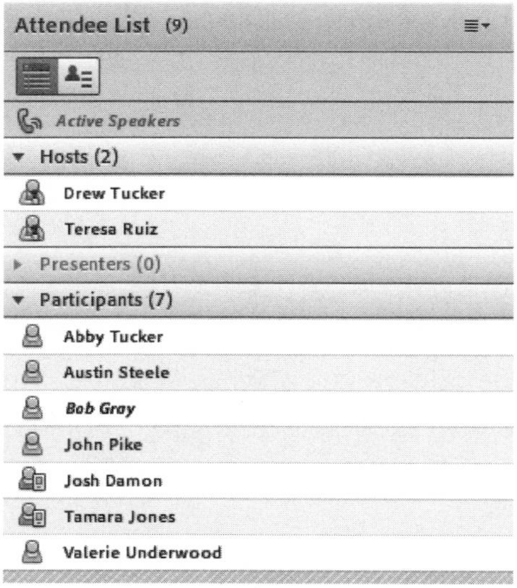

Figure 10-1 Adobe Connect attendee list with mobile participants.

> ## TIP
>
> Don't attempt to facilitate a session from a mobile device, as you won't have access to all the features of the virtual classroom, your audio quality may be poor, and you may lose connectivity.

Including participants who are using mobile devices introduces a new set of technical challenges. Since mobile participants need an Internet connection to participate, spotty data coverage or intermittent Wi-Fi service means that they may get accidentally dropped from a session. Participants who have data limits on their mobile device plans may get cut off from a session if they exceed their data limit.

Before attempting to include mobile participants in your session, test your session on a mobile device. Log in to the session from your mobile device, and walk all the way through to the end so you can see what adjustments need to be made to instructions, content, and exercises. The full set of features available for regular participants may not be available for mobile participants, or the features may work differently. Use Table 10-1 as a guide to note how the mobile app works.

If participants will join your session from a mobile device, here are a few items to keep in mind:

- Log in to your session from a mobile device, so you can watch the mobile "view" as you facilitate from your computer.
- Typing chat messages is slower on a mobile device than on a computer, so give mobile participants extra time to respond.
- Determine how you will handle audio for mobile participants: will they need to call a conference call or will they use VoIP?

Participants will also need a few additional instructions for the experience to go smoothly. You'll want to know ahead of time if anyone will join using a mobile device and if possible, walk them through the log in process and test their device with them in advance. Remind participants to:

- Charge their device before joining the session.
- Mute their device (Imagine the sound of an ambulance or wind blowing and disrupting the audio for everyone).
- Check Wi-Fi settings to locate a strong signal.

Mobile virtual classroom technology is still in its infancy, and I expect the tools and the market for these products to grow, introducing facilitators

Table 10-1 Virtual Classroom Mobile App Areas to Consider

Area	My Notes
What is the name of the mobile app in the app store?	
How do participants join a session from the mobile app?	
What size font on the slides is large enough to read on a mobile device?	
Does the content render differently when the device is held vertically and horizontally?	
When the facilitator uses drawing and pointer tools in the regular virtual classroom, does it display on the mobile app?	
How do participants type chat messages when using the mobile app?	
How do participants respond to poll questions when using the mobile app?	
How do participants provide instant feedback, such as raising a hand, when using the mobile app?	
Can participants see the instructor's webcam when using the mobile app?	

and participants to exciting new ways to connect from anywhere to learn together.

CONTINUOUS LEARNING

1. Brainstorm ideas on how you can use your virtual classroom tool for areas other than training.
2. Download the app for your virtual classroom tool and test the features.
3. Host a virtual session with coworkers or friends using mobile devices. Note how various devices performed during the session.

Glossary of Virtual Classroom Terms

Term	Definition
Bandwidth	Refers to the amount of data that can be transmitted from one point to another point over a computer network.
Blended Learning	Combining in-person training with technology-based training, such as self-paced e-learning or virtual classroom training.
Breakout Rooms	Private meeting subrooms that the facilitator creates for small group work. Participants can have small group discussions and collaborate on the whiteboard or chat.
Chat	A feature that allows participants and facilitators to send text messages in real time to chat publicly or privately with others in the classroom.
Drawing and Pointer Tools	A feature that allows the facilitator and participants to graphically mark up the screen in real time when a slide or whiteboard is displayed.
Facilitator	The main speaker who leads a virtual classroom session. May also be a subject matter expert.

Term	Definition
Firewall	A network security system that filters information coming through the Internet connection into a computer network. If an incoming packet of information is flagged by the filters because it doesn't meet the specified security criteria, it is not allowed through the firewall.
Instant Feedback	A feature that allows participants to communicate with facilitators at any time throughout a virtual classroom by selecting from a menu of feedback options, such as raise hand, agree, stepped away. Also referred to as a raise hand feature, status change, or emotion indicator.
Plug-In	A small downloadable application that adds a specific feature to an existing software application. Sometimes referred to as an add-on.
Poll	A feature that allows the facilitator to post questions to participants and show poll results in real time or after all responses have been received.
Producer	The virtual classroom technology expert who partners with the facilitator to deliver virtual classroom training.
Subject Matter Expert	An expert in a particular area or topic.
Screen Sharing	A feature that allows the facilitator or participant to share their own screen to show a website or other application such as Excel, with the class. Also referred to as application sharing.
Synchronous Learning	Scheduled learning that occurs in real time with a facilitator. May occur online in a virtual classroom or in-person in a traditional classroom.
Voice over Internet Protocol (VoIP)	Instead of using a phone, transmitting voice through the Internet (e.g., Skype).
Webinar	Short for a web-based seminar. Tends to be a one-way lecture or seminar with limited interactivity.
Webcam	A camera that is used to show live video over the web.
Webcast	A one-way presentation delivered over the web.
Whiteboard	A feature that allows for capturing of ideas/information by typing, highlighting, and drawing tools on a digital whiteboard.

APPENDIX B

Virtual Classroom Vendors

The virtual classroom marketplace is dynamic. A variety of vendors offer tools to host your virtual classroom, and popular virtual classroom vendors are listed below along with their product website and social media links. In addition to the virtual classroom vendors below, there are a variety of other products available to host web meetings.

Adobe Connect

Product Website: http://www.adobeconnect.com
Facebook: https://www.facebook.com/adobeconnect
LinkedIn User Group: http://www.linkedin.com/groups/
    Adobe-Connect-Users-718517
Twitter: @AdobeConnect
User Community: http://www.connectusers.com/

Blackboard Collaborate

Product Website: http://www.blackboardcollaborate.com
Facebook: https://www.facebook.com/blackboard
LinkedIn Company Page: http://www.linkedin.com/company/blackboard

Twitter: @Blackboard
User Community (independent): http://www.wecollaborate.com/

Cisco WebEx

Product Website: http://www.webex.com
Facebook: https://www.facebook.com/webex
LinkedIn Company Page: http://www.linkedin.com/company/webex
Twitter: @WebEx

Citrix GoToMeeting, GoToTraining and GoToWebinar

Product Website: http://www.gotomeeting.com
Facebook: https://www.facebook.com/Citrix
LinkedIn Company Page: http://www.linkedin.com/company/citrix
Twitter: @Citrix
User Community: http://community.gotomeeting.com/

Saba Classroom

Product Website: http://www.saba.com/sabameeting/
    virtual-classroom-software/
Facebook: https://www.facebook.com/SabaSoftware
LinkedIn: https://www.linkedin.com/company/saba
Twitter: @SabaSoftware
User Community: http://community.sabapeoplecloud.com

Feature List to Consider When Selecting a Virtual Classroom Tool

If you are selecting a virtual classroom tool, review the business requirements the virtual training is intended to address. Then, ask yourself what are the primary types of training sessions you will conduct. Identify which features of the virtual classroom will be most important to deliver a successful session. Some areas to consider are highlighted below.

Features	Notes
Annotation and Drawing Tools	
Types of drawing tools included	
Drawing tools may be opened up to participants	
Audio	
Supports Voice over Internet Protocol (VoIP)	
Includes integrated conference call	
Includes dial-back audio	

Features	Notes
Breakout Rooms	
Maximum number of breakout rooms	
Maximum number of participants per breakout room	
Audio options for breakout rooms	
Chat	
Allows for both public and private chat	
Ability to export chat after session concludes	
Customization/Branding of Interface	
Ability to customize or log in registration or screens	
Concurrent Users	
Maximum number of participants per meeting	
Maximum number of presenters per meeting	
Event Management	
Ability to send invitations to audience	
Ability to track enrollment and completion	
Language	
Language interface options (other than English)	
Mobile Device Support	
Types of mobile devices and tablets supported	
Persistent Meeting Rooms	
Ability to reuse a meeting room	
Polling	
Question types supported (multiple choice, multiple answer)	
Ability to preload polls	
Ability to run multiple polls simultaneously	

Features	Notes
Plug-Ins	
Plug-Ins or other installation required for participants, hosts (e.g., Java, FlashPlayer, etc.)	
Pricing Structure	
Pricing per user, per license, per minute, etc.	
Recording	
Ability to record a session	
Ability to edit the recording	
Ability to export recording	
Registrations/Event Management	
Integration with calendaring tool	
Integration with Learning Management System (LMS)	
Integration with instant messaging tool	
Ability to track registrations and attendance	
Reports	
Types of postmeeting reports	
Ability to export reports into other formats (Excel, etc)	
Section 508 Compliance	
Features that allow for people with disabilities to use the software	
Screen Sharing (or Application Sharing)	
Ability to share entire desktop or just one screen	
Status Change Icons	
Ability for participants to raise hand, emoticons, stepped away, etc.	

Features	Notes
Supported File Types	
File types that can be loaded and shared in a meeting (slides, audio files, video files)	
System Requirements	
Requirements for hosting or licensing	
Video Support	
Ability to incorporate webcams, video feeds	
Whiteboard	
Ability to draw on a whiteboard using text or drawing tools	
My Additional Requirements	

Virtual Classroom Resources

Books

Barclay, Ph.D., Kathleen, Al Gordon, Jim Hollahan, and Yatman Lai. *The Live E-Learning Cookbook*. Lincoln, NE: iUniverse, Inc., 2003.

Clay, Cynthia. *Great Webinars*. San Francisco, CA: Pfeiffer, 2012.

Courville, Roger. *The Virtual Presenter's Handbook*. Troutdale, OR: 1080 Group LLC, 2009.

Hofmann, Jennifer. *The Synchronous Trainer's Survival Guide*. San Francisco, CA: Pfeiffer, 2004.

Huggett, Cindy. *Virtual Training Basics*. Alexandria, VA: ASTD Press, 2010.

Huggett, Cindy. *The Virtual Training Guidebook*. Alexandria, VA: ASTD Press, 2014.

Pluth, Becky. *Webinars with WOW Factor*. Pluth Consulting, 2010.

Pluth, Becky Pike, et al. *SCORE for Webinar Training*. Creative Training Productions, 2014.

Turmel, Wayne. *10 Steps to Successful Virtual Presentations*. Alexandria, VA: ASTD Press, 2011.

Other Publications

Christopher, Darlene. "Facilitating in the Global Virtual Classroom." *ASTD Infoline*, Alexandria, VA: ASTD Press, November 2011.

Corbett, Wendy Gates and Cindy Huggett. "Designing for the Virtual Classroom." *ASTD Infoline*, Alexandria, VA: ASTD Press, November 2009.

Corbett, Wendy Gates and Cindy Huggett. "Simple, Effective Online Training." *ASTD Infoline,* Alexandria, VA: ASTD Press, January 2008.

Edmundson, Andrea. "Training for Multiple Cultures." *ASTD Infoline*, Alexandria, VA: ASTD Press, February 2010.

Hyder, Karen, et al. *The eLearning Guild's Handbook on Synchronous e-Learning*. Santa Rosa, CA: The eLearning Guild, 2007.

Wexler, Steve, et al. *360 Synchronous Learning Systems*. Santa Rosa, CA: The eLearning Guild, 2007.

Professional Associations and Organizations

American Society for Training and Development / Association for Talent Development

http://www.astd.org/
LinkedIn Group: ASTD National
Facebook: https://www.facebook.com/pages/
ASTD-International/127572753956944
Twitter: @astd

Brandon Hall Group

http://brandon-hall.com/
Facebook: https://www.facebook.com/groups/5854362723/
LinkedIn Group: Brandon Hall Research Innovations in Learning
Twitter: @ BrandonHallGrp

Chief Learning Officer

http://www.clomedia.com/
Facebook: https://www.facebook.com/clomedia

LinkedIn Group: Chief Learning Officer magazine
Twitter: @clomedia

Distance Educator

http://www.distance-educator.com/
Facebook: https://www.facebook.com/distanceeducator
Twitter: @distance_e

The eLearning Guild

http://www.elearningguild.com/
Facebook: https://www.facebook.com/pages/
    The-eLearning-Guild/265302656953
LinkedIn Group: The eLearning Guild
Twitter: @eLearningGuild

MASIE Center Learning Lab

http://www.masie.com/
Twitter: @emasie

Society for Applied Learning Technology

http://www.salt.org/
Facebook: https://www.facebook.com/SocietyforAppliedLearningTechnology
LinkedIn Group: Society for Applied Learning (SALT)
Twitter: @saltlti

United States Distance Learning Association

http://www.usdla.org/
Facebook: https://www.facebook.com/groups/usdla/
LinkedIn Group: United States Distance Learning Association
Twitter: @usdla

Global Resources

European Distance and E-Learning Network

http://www.eden-online.org/
Facebook: https://www.facebook.com/pages/
    European-Distance-and-E-learning-Network-EDEN/144392062298793
Twitter: @EDEN20_Official

The Global E-Learning Community

http://the-gec.org/
LinkedIn Group: Global eLearning Community

Example of Course Conversion

Example of a Writing Class Converted from Face-to-Face to Virtual Classroom

	Face-to-Face Classroom	Virtual Classroom	Notes
Enrollment	Closed one week before class start date.	Closed three weeks before class start date.	Needed extra time to physically mail materials to participants.
Class Size	Up to 20.	Up to 12.	Reduced class size to accommodate design that called for more exercises as an entire group instead of small groups.
Facilitation Team	Facilitator supported by a course administrator.	Facilitator supported by course administrator and producer.	A producer partnered with facilitator to manage the virtual classroom technology.
Environment	Participants and facilitator in a conference room in a single location.	Participants and facilitator in a virtual classroom from multiple countries.	Used teleconference for audio.

	Face-to-Face Classroom	**Virtual Classroom**	**Notes**
Duration	One 7-hour session.	Session 1: three hours. Session 2: three hours.	Broke course into 2 sessions. Trimmed non-essential content from the face-to-face session so everything could be covered in 2 sessions.
PowerPoint Slides	40 slides.	Session 1: 90 slides. Session 2: 65 slides.	Added slides such as an agenda, images of facilitators, participants, materials, exercise instructions, transitions, among others.
Participant Materials	Workbook, job aid, answer sheets handed out in class.	Materials physically mailed to participants in advance.	Took photos of materials and included in slides, added workbook page numbers to slides. Included virtual class-room instructions and table with photos of participants and facilitators.
Exercises	Plenary discussions, small group discussions, individual exercises in workbook.	Plenary discussions, individual exercises in workbook, partner chat, polling exercises.	Adjusted exercises to utilize the virtual classroom features.
Writing Sample	Participants email a writing sample and instructor edits. Printed copies brought to room.	Participants email a writing sample and instructor edits; elec-tronic copy posted in meeting room.	Instructor chatted individually with each participant to share comments on writing sample.
Evaluation	Paper evaluation handed out at end of course.	Electronic evaluation completed at the end of the session.	Posted a Survey Monkey link in chat.

Webcam Tips

If you will use a webcam in your virtual classroom session, here are some tips to keep in mind.

Connection Speed/Bandwidth

The ability of your computer to smoothly stream audio and your webcam during a virtual classroom session depends, in part, on your bandwidth or connection to the Internet. Additionally, Wi-Fi connections may be slower and less stable than a hardwired connection directly to a router. To select the ideal streaming settings (voice only or voice and video), test your connection speed with a mock audience to get feedback. Can they hear and see you clearly without any choppy (out of sync audio/video feeds) or delayed audio or video streaming? If your bandwidth does not allow for smooth streaming, consider forgoing streaming your webcam and stick only with audio. Note that the ability of participants to view your video and audio stream may depend on *their* connection to the Internet, so test with various individuals in different locations.

Professional Background

Remember you will be projecting not only your face to your audience, but whatever is behind you. To prevent unnecessary distraction, make sure the background behind you is professional. Don't make your kid's artwork or a cluttered home environment the central feature of your virtual session background. If your home or office doesn't offer an ideal environment, consider purchasing a privacy screen that blocks out distraction (http://www.gadgetsgo .com/logitech-creative-usb-home-office-cam-pc-cover.html).

Lighting

Ensure the lighting is adequate on your face. Don't sit in front of a window if it's bright outside as your face will appear too dark on camera. If you rely only on ceiling lights, you will get shadows under your eyes and nose, so try to get an adjustable light that shines on your face.

Positioning

Sit a comfortable distance away from your computer screen so as not to appear too close. A good rule of thumb is to sit at an arms' length away from your computer screen, which will allow viewers to see your head, shoulders, and midsection.

Movement

Try to keep your movement to a minimum when you speak. If you have a webcam that has "motion control" that follows you as you move, disable this feature to prevent you from projecting a waving/moving image which may make your audience seasick.

Clothing and Accessories

Wear solid, neutral colors, and avoid busy patterns like stripes and plaids. Avoid dangling jewelry that creates a distraction and bracelets that create noise if they hit your desk or keyboard as you move your mouse or type.

Rehearsal Feedback Form

Please give the facilitation team feedback on improving the virtual classroom session.

1. Date _____ Session Title _____

2. Name_____ Email_____

3. Mark an X in the box to rate the pace of each section of the session

Section	Too Slow	About Right	Too Fast
Opening			
Topic 1 [name]			
Topic 2 [name]			
Topic 3 [name]			
Closing			

Additional comments: _____

4. Mark an X in the box that describes your reaction to the statements below about the clarity of the session:

	Strongly Disagree	Disagree	Neutral	Agree	Strongly Agree
[Name] spoke clearly.					
[Name] spoke clearly.					
The slides were clear.					
I understood what was expected of me in the exercises.					
The participant workbook was clear.					

Additional comments: _____

5. What did you like most about this session?

6. What two things would you recommend improving?

7. Did you experience any technical difficulties? If so, please explain.

8. (OPTIONAL) Share your feedback on making this training culturally appropriate for participants from [target county names].

Were there any examples, references used that didn't make sense (people, places, slang, local humor, etc.). If so, name items to change and give a suggested change, if you have one.

Item to Change	Suggested Change
1.	1.
2.	2.
3.	3.
4.	4
5.	5.

PREP Model Checklist

PREP (Plan, Rehearse, Execute, Postsession Review) Checklist

PLAN **Learn Platform**

✓ Identify the virtual classroom tool (software application) that best suits your training needs.
✓ Learn the features and functionality of the tool and how they work.
✓ Understand the limitations of the tool (maximum number of participants, hosts, etc.)
✓ Understand audio options available (VoIP, integrated conference call).

Select Facilitation Team and Roles

✓ Identify a facilitator who knows how to engage virtual participants.
✓ Identify an instructional designer who has experience with virtual classroom design.
✓ Identify a producer to partner with the facilitator.
✓ Determine division of labor and roles between the facilitator and producer.
✓ Select a course administrator to handle event planning.
✓ Identify IT support.

Prepare Content, Interactivity Exercises, and Guides

✓ Divide content into prework and postwork, leaving discussion and topics that require a facilitator's input for the time spent in the virtual classroom session.
✓ Incorporate features of the virtual classroom into the design appropriately, with interactivity every 3 to 5 minutes (e.g., polls, whiteboarding chat, exercises).
✓ Offer a variety of exercises that appeal to different learning styles and personalities.
✓ Develop slides that cover one key concept each and include appropriate images, videos and other instructional materials.

✓   Develop a facilitator guide that describes what material will be covered as each slide or other content appears, actions the facilitator and producer will take, and a detailed timeline.

✓   Develop participant workbooks and other supporting materials that are clear, consistent, and accurate.

Organize Logistics

✓   Select session start and end times that match the working hours and work days of participants.

✓   Send course materials to participants with instructions on how to access them.

✓   Identify optimal audio option for training (VoIP, integrated conference call).

✓   Select audio transmission type (teleconference, VoIP) and test with the facilitation team and participants.

✓   Secure a location and equipment for the facilitation team to use to deliver the session.

REHEARSE

✓   Rehearse with facilitation team (i.e., facilitator and producer), so all are clear on who does what, who says what, and the timing of content/exercises.

✓   Rehearse in front of a mock audience to verify that the content is clear and the exercises make sense.

✓   Test audio transmission (teleconference, VoIP) with the facilitation team and mock audience.

✓   Rehearse in the location that will be used for the formal launch.

✓   Practice the first three minutes until they are flawless and energetic to set a positive tone for the session.

✓   Fix the problem areas identified during rehearsal (e.g., update slides or correct the facilitator guide).

EXECUTE

✓   Log in 30 minutes early and encourage participants to log in early (5 to 10 minutes).

✓   Ensure that the virtual classroom session starts and ends on time.

✓   Engage the audience early, exposing the audience to the variety of methods they can use to interact.

✓   Give participants enough time to respond to questions, polls, chat (brief silence is okay!).

✓   Place an extra computer next to the facilitator's computer to see the participant "view" at all times.

✓   Implement back-up plans in case something goes wrong (back-up computers, headsets, screen shots, etc.).

POSTSESSION

✓   Gather feedback from participants at the end of the session or immediately following the session.

✓   Debrief the session with the facilitation team shortly after it ends.

✓   Download the chat text and review, convert into an FAQ if appropriate.

Index

About the Author

Darlene Christopher has designed and delivered virtual training programs for global audiences for ten years, has authored numerous articles on virtual training, and is a contributing author to the *ASTD Handbook,* 2nd ed., *Road Tested, SCORE! For Webinar Training,* and the *2012 Pfeiffer Annual Training.* She is a Knowledge & Learning Officer for The World Bank in Washington, DC, where she directs regional learning programs for staff and provides technical leadership on distance learning programs for international government institutions. Previously, Darlene held technology development and management positions at Disney Internet Group, 3Com, and Nextel. Darlene has an MPA in International Management from the Monterey Institute of International Studies and a BA in Spanish from the University of California, Davis.

Darlene blogs at www.darlenechristopher.com. You can also connect with her on Twitter: @darlenec.

The findings, interpretations, and conclusions expressed in this publication are those of the author(s) and should not be attributed in any manner to The World Bank, its Board of Executive Directors, or the governments it represents.